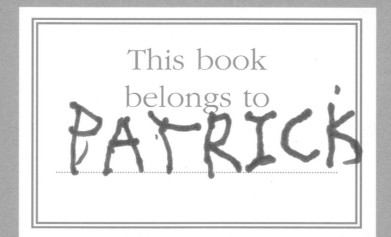

This book
belongs to
PATRICK

PATRICK

First Atlas

Written and designed by

Nicola Wright · Tony Potter · Dee Turner · Christine Wilson

Illustrated by

Lyn Mitchell

Contents

All about maps	2	Africa	24
World map	4	U.S.S.R.	26
The United States of America	6	The Middle East	28
		South Asia	30
State flags	8	Southeast Asia	32
About the United States	10	East Asia	34
North America	14	Australia and New Zealand	36
South America	16	Arctic	38
Northern Europe	18	Antarctic	39
Britain and Central Europe	20	Index	40
Mediterranean Europe	22		

SMITHMARK

All about maps

A map is a picture of a place from above. Imagine what your home would look like if you flew over it in an airplane and took a photograph. The picture would show the area around your home spread out flat.

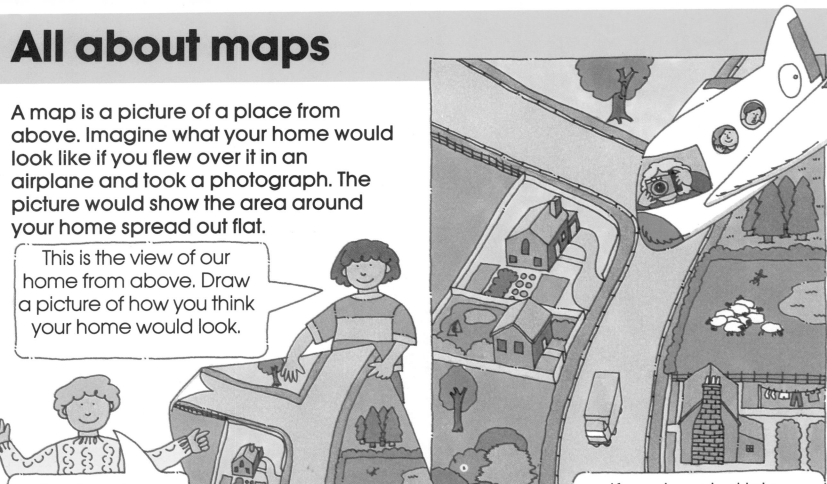

This is the view of our home from above. Draw a picture of how you think your home would look.

See how the picture shows the houses, trees, and roads.

If you traveled into space you would see other countries as well as your island.

My town

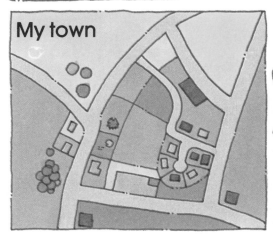

My island

The Earth

Imagine that you fly higher. Now you can see your whole town or city. Everything looks tiny.

Imagine your town is on an island. As you go even higher you can see the whole island.

Clouds form in the sky and swirl around the Earth. There is much more ocean than land.

This is how my island would look as a map. Tiny pictures called symbols are used to stand for real things.

2

The pictures below are the symbols used in this book. This part of an atlas is called the **legend**. The legend tells you what the symbols stand for.

Looking for a country? Here is what to do: Go to the list on page 40 and look under the first letter of the country name. So, **Chile** is under the letter **C**.

 **Country boundaries**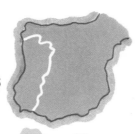

 **Oceans and Seas**

 **Capital cities** ■ Moscow

Large cities ● Vladivostok

 **Lakes**

Rivers

 **High mountains**

Low mountains

 **Tropical rain forest**

 **Monsoon woodland** (hot areas with a rainy season)

 **Pine forest**

 **Leafy woodland**

Mixed woodland

 **Mediterranean woodland** (dry areas with evergreen trees)

Desert (some deserts are just sandy, but some are stony and covered with bushes or cacti)

Grassland (called **prairie** in North America, and **pampas** in South America)

Steppe (scrubland or grassland in Asia)

Savannah (dry grasslands with some trees in Africa)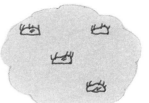

Tundra (frozen land)

Ice

World map

This big map shows the world as though its round shape has been flattened out. The differently colored areas of land are called continents. There are seven continents and four oceans.

This is planet Earth. Imagine a line around its middle. This is called the equator.

This book shows you some of the people, animals, plants, and places found in each continent.

The biggest continent is Asia. The smallest continent is Australia.

Countries

The maps in this book show all the countries in the world. A white line shows where one country joins another.

Every country has a flag. Some of them are shown in this book.

The Polish flag

The Belgian flag

The Portugese flag

Italian flag.

Arctic Ocean

North America

Atlantic Ocean

Equator

Pacific Ocean

South America

Atlantic Ocean

The bottom half of the world is called the southern hemisphere.

SOUTH POLE

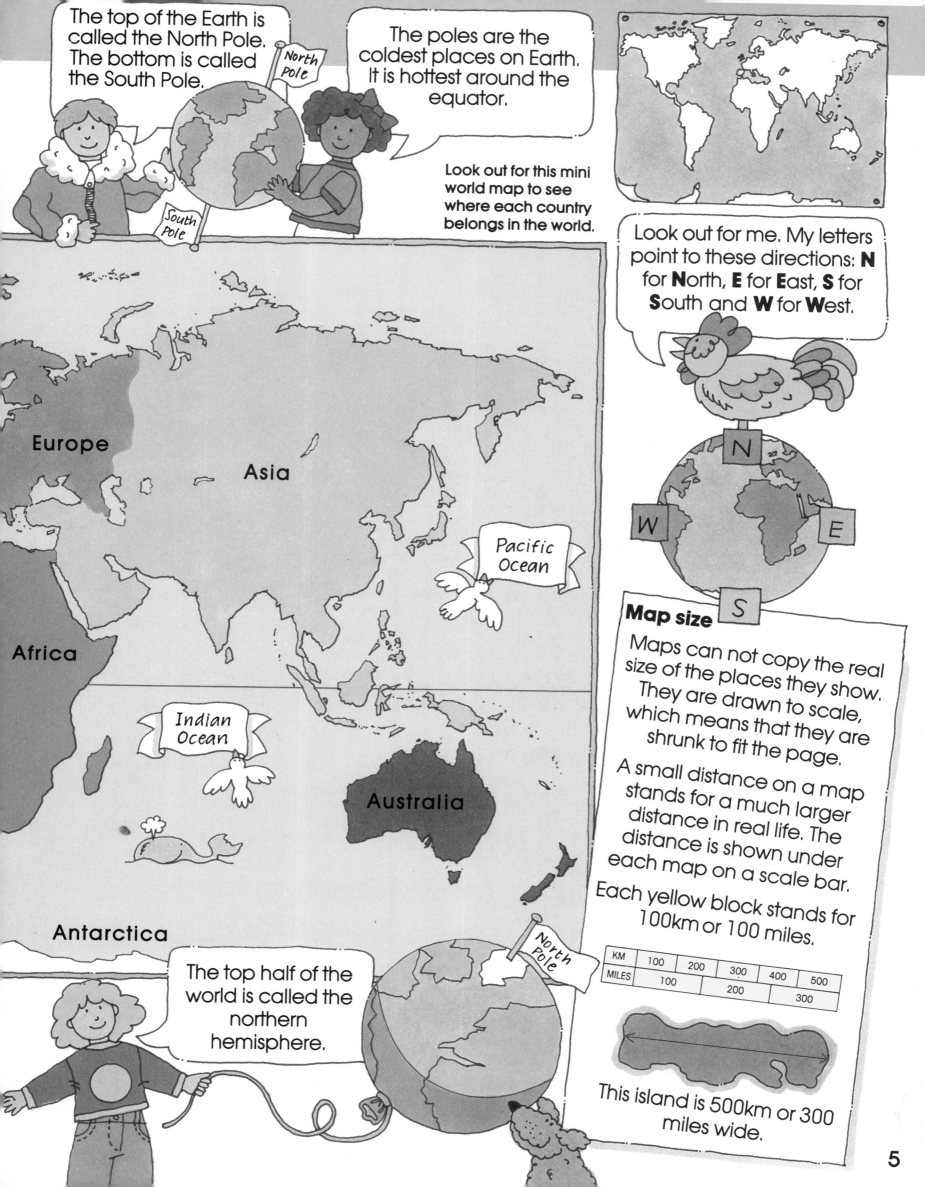

The United States of America

The United States of America is divided into 50 separate states and the District of Columbia. Here you can see each state's boundary and capital city.

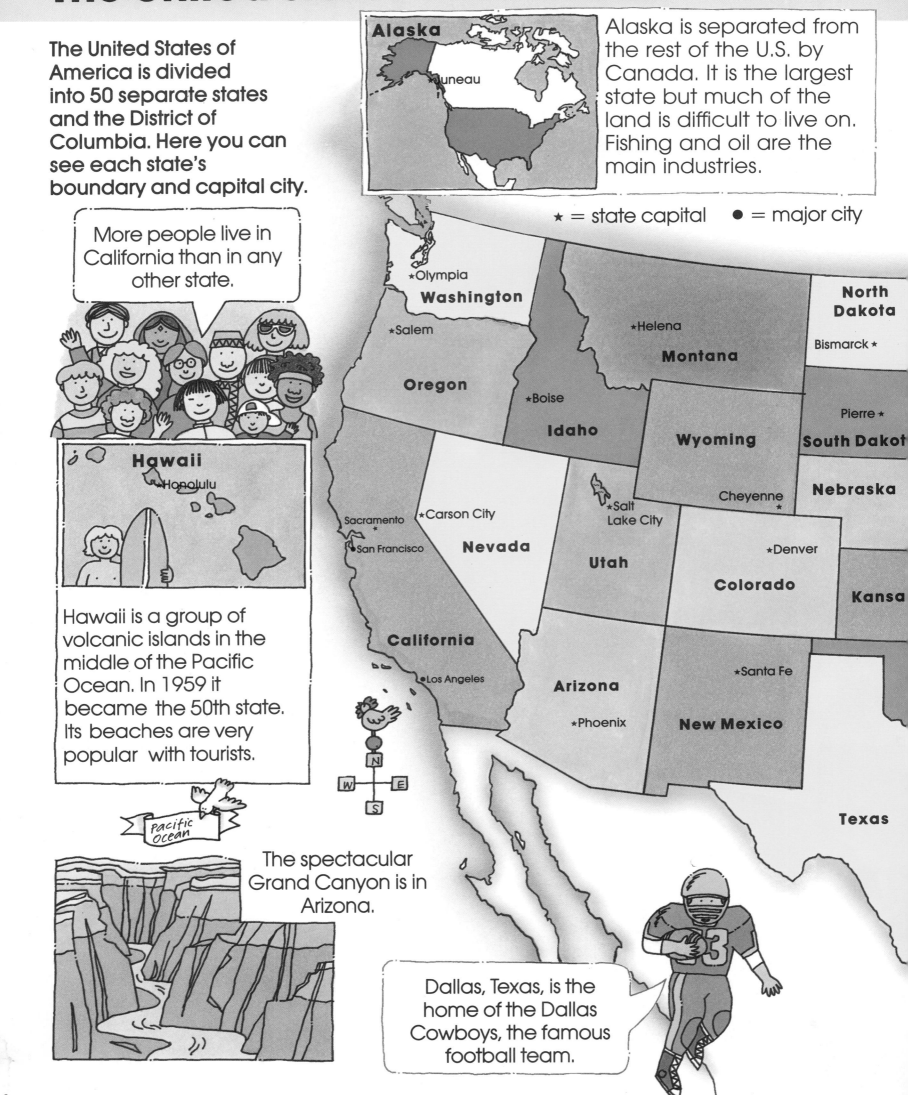

Alaska
★Juneau

Alaska is separated from the rest of the U.S. by Canada. It is the largest state but much of the land is difficult to live on. Fishing and oil are the main industries.

More people live in California than in any other state.

★ = state capital   ● = major city

Hawaii
★Honolulu

Hawaii is a group of volcanic islands in the middle of the Pacific Ocean. In 1959 it became the 50th state. Its beaches are very popular with tourists.

Pacific Ocean

★Olympia
Washington
★Salem
Oregon
★Boise
Idaho
★Helena
Montana
North Dakota
Bismarck ★
Pierre ★
South Dakot
Wyoming
Cheyenne ★
Nebraska
★Salt Lake City
Sacramento ★
★Carson City
●San Francisco
Nevada
Utah
★Denver
Colorado
Kansa
California
●Los Angeles
★Santa Fe
Arizona
★Phoenix
New Mexico

N
W   E
S

Texas

The spectacular Grand Canyon is in Arizona.

Dallas, Texas, is the home of the Dallas Cowboys, the famous football team.

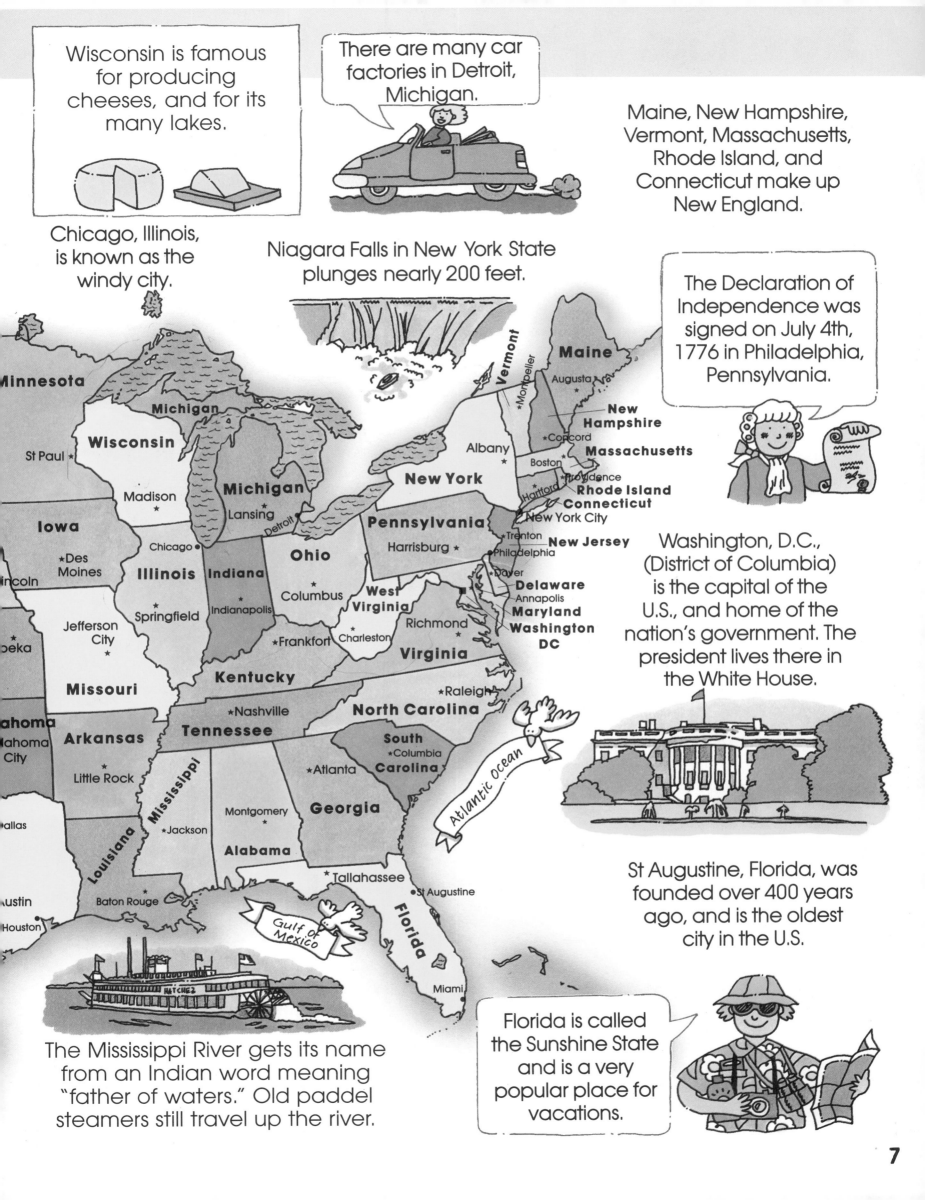

Wisconsin is famous for producing cheeses, and for its many lakes.

There are many car factories in Detroit, Michigan.

Maine, New Hampshire, Vermont, Massachusetts, Rhode Island, and Connecticut make up New England.

Chicago, Illinois, is known as the windy city.

Niagara Falls in New York State plunges nearly 200 feet.

The Declaration of Independence was signed on July 4th, 1776 in Philadelphia, Pennsylvania.

Washington, D.C., (District of Columbia) is the capital of the U.S., and home of the nation's government. The president lives there in the White House.

St Augustine, Florida, was founded over 400 years ago, and is the oldest city in the U.S.

The Mississippi River gets its name from an Indian word meaning "father of waters." Old paddel steamers still travel up the river.

Florida is called the Sunshine State and is a very popular place for vacations.

Minnesota
Michigan
Wisconsin
St Paul ★
Madison ★
Michigan
Lansing ★
Iowa
Des Moines ★
Chicago ●
Illinois
Indiana
Ohio
Columbus ★
West Virginia
Pennsylvania
Harrisburg ★
New York
Albany ★
Vermont
Montpelier ★
Maine
Augusta ★
New Hampshire
Concord ★
Massachusetts
Boston ★
Providence ★
Rhode Island
Hartford ★
Connecticut
New York City
Trenton ★
New Jersey
Philadelphia ●
Dover ★
Delaware
Annapolis ★
Maryland
Washington DC
lincoln
Springfield ★
Indianapolis ★
Frankfort ★
Charleston ★
Richmond ★
Virginia
Jefferson City ★
peka ★
Missouri
Kentucky
Nashville ★
Raleigh ★
North Carolina
ahoma
ahoma City
Arkansas
Little Rock ★
Tennessee
South Carolina
Columbia ★
Atlanta ★
Georgia
Mississippi
Jackson ★
Montgomery ★
Alabama
Louisiana
Baton Rouge ★
allas
ustin
Houston ●
Tallahassee ★
St Augustine ●
Florida
Miami ●
Gulf of Mexico
Atlantic Ocean
HATCHEZ

State flags

Each state has its own capital city, flag, bird, flower, tree, and even song. Here you can see all fifty different state flags. This is what the little pictures beside the flags mean:

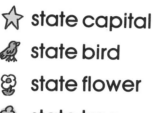 state capital

state bird

state flower

state tree

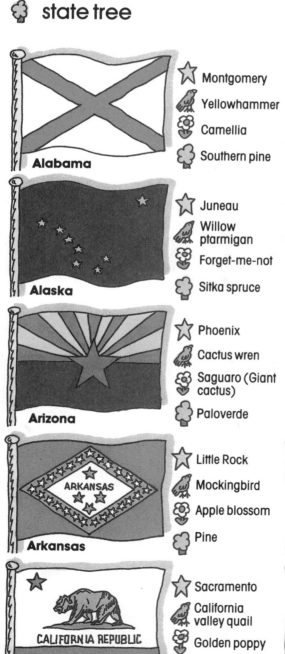

Alabama
- Montgomery
- Yellowhammer
- Camellia
- Southern pine

Alaska
- Juneau
- Willow ptarmigan
- Forget-me-not
- Sitka spruce

Arizona
- Phoenix
- Cactus wren
- Saguaro (Giant cactus)
- Paloverde

Arkansas
- Little Rock
- Mockingbird
- Apple blossom
- Pine

California
- Sacramento
- California valley quail
- Golden poppy
- California redwood

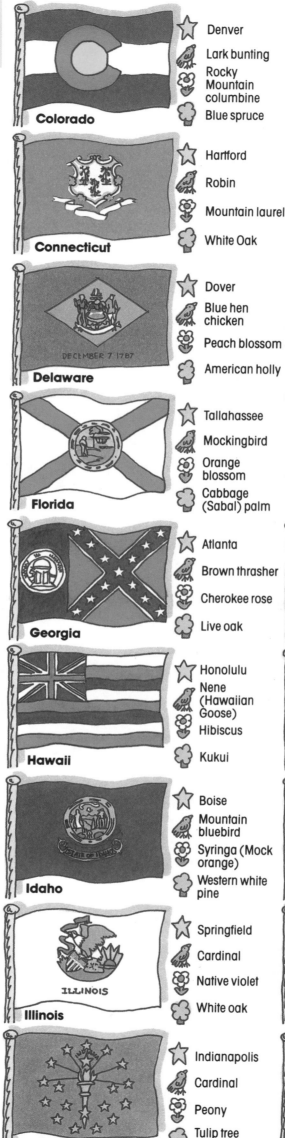

Colorado
- Denver
- Lark bunting
- Rocky Mountain columbine
- Blue spruce

Connecticut
- Hartford
- Robin
- Mountain laurel
- White Oak

Delaware
- Dover
- Blue hen chicken
- Peach blossom
- American holly

Florida
- Tallahassee
- Mockingbird
- Orange blossom
- Cabbage (Sabal) palm

Georgia
- Atlanta
- Brown thrasher
- Cherokee rose
- Live oak

Hawaii
- Honolulu
- Nene (Hawaiian Goose)
- Hibiscus
- Kukui

Idaho
- Boise
- Mountain bluebird
- Syringa (Mock orange)
- Western white pine

Illinois
- Springfield
- Cardinal
- Native violet
- White oak

Indiana
- Indianapolis
- Cardinal
- Peony
- Tulip tree (Yellow poplar)

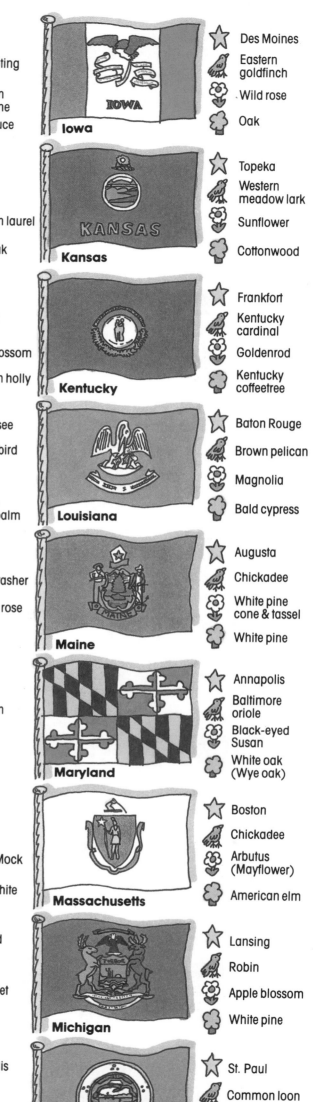

Iowa
- Des Moines
- Eastern goldfinch
- Wild rose
- Oak

Kansas
- Topeka
- Western meadow lark
- Sunflower
- Cottonwood

Kentucky
- Frankfort
- Kentucky cardinal
- Goldenrod
- Kentucky coffeetree

Louisiana
- Baton Rouge
- Brown pelican
- Magnolia
- Bald cypress

Maine
- Augusta
- Chickadee
- White pine cone & tassel
- White pine

Maryland
- Annapolis
- Baltimore oriole
- Black-eyed Susan
- White oak (Wye oak)

Massachusetts
- Boston
- Chickadee
- Arbutus (Mayflower)
- American elm

Michigan
- Lansing
- Robin
- Apple blossom
- White pine

Minnesota
- St. Paul
- Common loon
- Pink & white lady's-slipper
- Norway, or red, pine

8

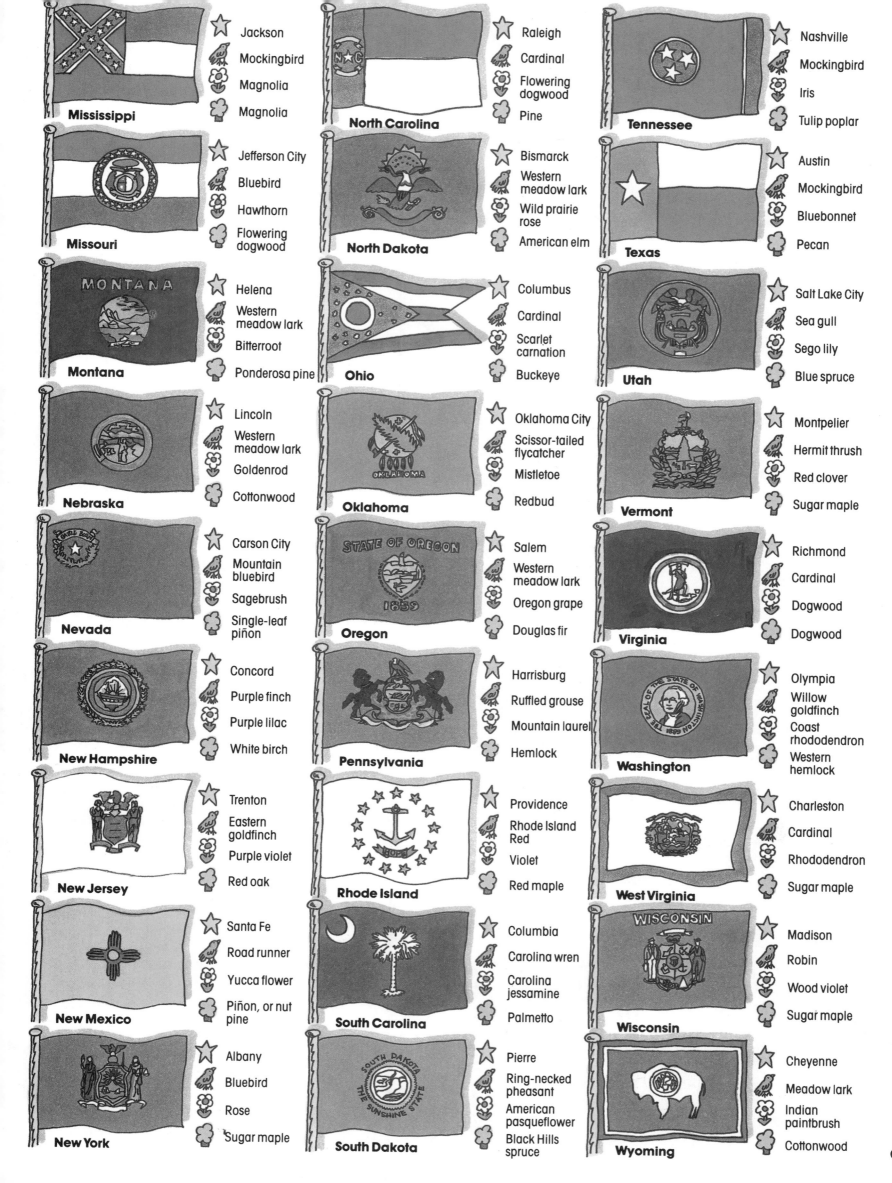

Mississippi
- ⭐ Jackson
- 🐦 Mockingbird
- 🌸 Magnolia
- 🌳 Magnolia

Missouri
- ⭐ Jefferson City
- 🐦 Bluebird
- 🌸 Hawthorn
- 🌳 Flowering dogwood

Montana
- ⭐ Helena
- 🐦 Western meadow lark
- 🌸 Bitterroot
- 🌳 Ponderosa pine

Nebraska
- ⭐ Lincoln
- 🐦 Western meadow lark
- 🌸 Goldenrod
- 🌳 Cottonwood

Nevada
- ⭐ Carson City
- 🐦 Mountain bluebird
- 🌸 Sagebrush
- 🌳 Single-leaf piñon

New Hampshire
- ⭐ Concord
- 🐦 Purple finch
- 🌸 Purple lilac
- 🌳 White birch

New Jersey
- ⭐ Trenton
- 🐦 Eastern goldfinch
- 🌸 Purple violet
- 🌳 Red oak

New Mexico
- ⭐ Santa Fe
- 🐦 Road runner
- 🌸 Yucca flower
- 🌳 Piñon, or nut pine

New York
- ⭐ Albany
- 🐦 Bluebird
- 🌸 Rose
- 🌳 Sugar maple

North Carolina
- ⭐ Raleigh
- 🐦 Cardinal
- 🌸 Flowering dogwood
- 🌳 Pine

North Dakota
- ⭐ Bismarck
- 🐦 Western meadow lark
- 🌸 Wild prairie rose
- 🌳 American elm

Ohio
- ⭐ Columbus
- 🐦 Cardinal
- 🌸 Scarlet carnation
- 🌳 Buckeye

Oklahoma
- ⭐ Oklahoma City
- 🐦 Scissor-tailed flycatcher
- 🌸 Mistletoe
- 🌳 Redbud

Oregon
- ⭐ Salem
- 🐦 Western meadow lark
- 🌸 Oregon grape
- 🌳 Douglas fir

Pennsylvania
- ⭐ Harrisburg
- 🐦 Ruffled grouse
- 🌸 Mountain laurel
- 🌳 Hemlock

Rhode Island
- ⭐ Providence
- 🐦 Rhode Island Red
- 🌸 Violet
- 🌳 Red maple

South Carolina
- ⭐ Columbia
- 🐦 Carolina wren
- 🌸 Carolina jessamine
- 🌳 Palmetto

South Dakota
- ⭐ Pierre
- 🐦 Ring-necked pheasant
- 🌸 American pasqueflower
- 🌳 Black Hills spruce

Tennessee
- ⭐ Nashville
- 🐦 Mockingbird
- 🌸 Iris
- 🌳 Tulip poplar

Texas
- ⭐ Austin
- 🐦 Mockingbird
- 🌸 Bluebonnet
- 🌳 Pecan

Utah
- ⭐ Salt Lake City
- 🐦 Sea gull
- 🌸 Sego lily
- 🌳 Blue spruce

Vermont
- ⭐ Montpelier
- 🐦 Hermit thrush
- 🌸 Red clover
- 🌳 Sugar maple

Virginia
- ⭐ Richmond
- 🐦 Cardinal
- 🌸 Dogwood
- 🌳 Dogwood

Washington
- ⭐ Olympia
- 🐦 Willow goldfinch
- 🌸 Coast rhododendron
- 🌳 Western hemlock

West Virginia
- ⭐ Charleston
- 🐦 Cardinal
- 🌸 Rhododendron
- 🌳 Sugar maple

Wisconsin
- ⭐ Madison
- 🐦 Robin
- 🌸 Wood violet
- 🌳 Sugar maple

Wyoming
- ⭐ Cheyenne
- 🐦 Meadow lark
- 🌸 Indian paintbrush
- 🌳 Cottonwood

9

About the United States

There are four main parts of the U.S. called regions – the Northeast, South, Midwest, and West. Each region differs from the others in many ways, such as weather, animals, plants and trees, farming, industry, and places of interest. The West is the largest region, and the Northeast is the smallest.

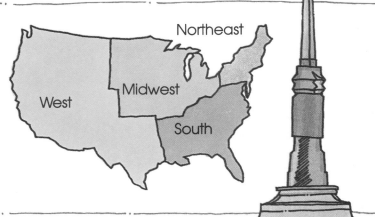

The Northeast

The many natural harbors, lakes, and rivers attracted settlers to this region. People from all over the world still arrive at its ports to begin a new life in the United States.

Summers are usually hot and damp, but the winters are quite cold.

New York Harbor

Most of the people of this region live in cities.

New York is the most crowded city in the the United States. Twice as many people visit it each year as live there. It is also one of the world's three major business centers.

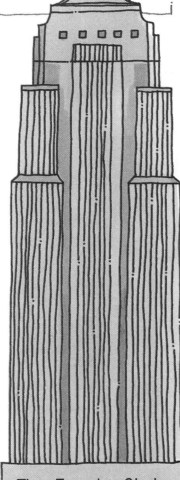

The Empire State Building is very popular with tourists.

There are many hills and mountain ranges.

Beavers, weasels, deer, and porcupines live in the forests.

The South

The sandy beaches of the South make it a good place for vacations. It is also a big farming area, producing tobacco, soybeans, cotton, and peanuts.

Walt Disney World in Orlando, Florida, is a giant amusement park.

Kentucky and Virginia are famous for breeding fine horses.

Nashville, Tennessee, is the national capital for country music.

Traditional Southern dishes include cornbread, grits and gumbo.

Atlanta, Georgia, has one of the busiest airports in the country.

Twenty-five kinds of snakes live in the Everglades National Park, Florida.

Alligators are found in the swamplands.

Skunks, opossums, and snakes live in the South.

The Midwest

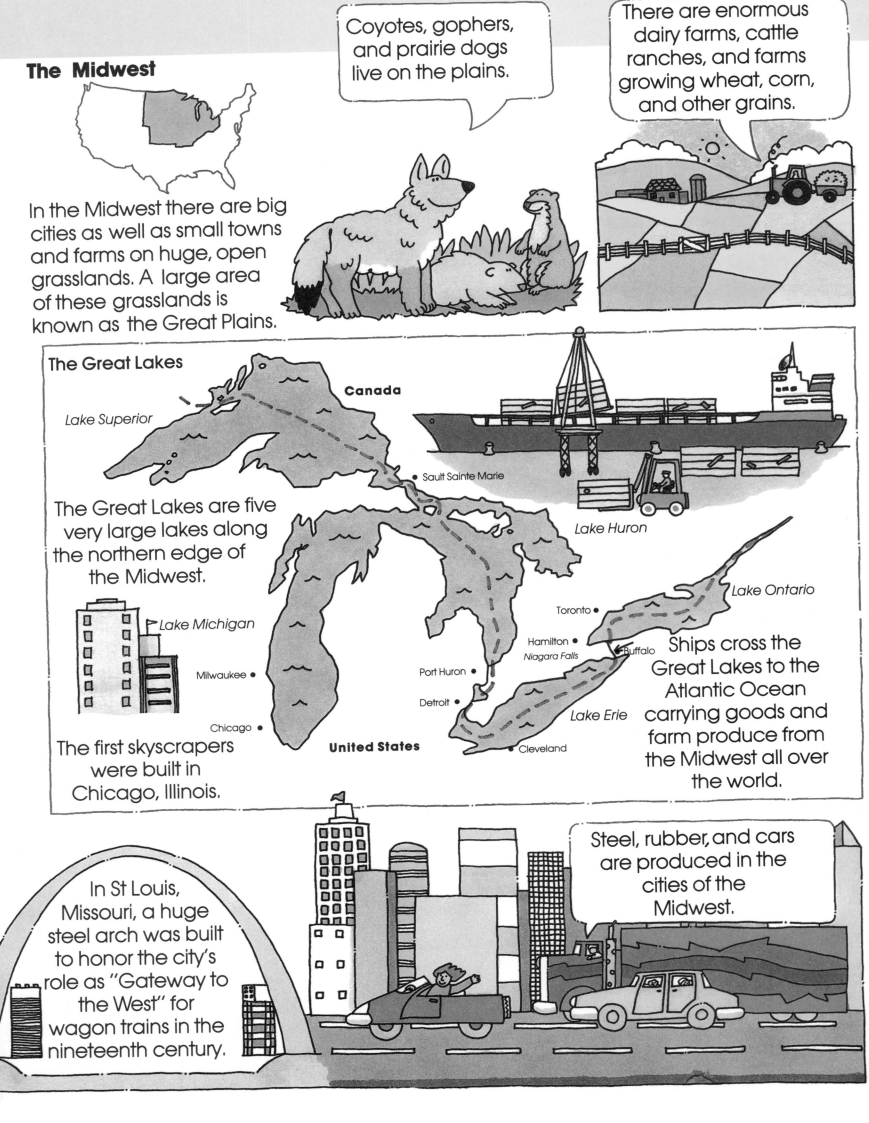

In the Midwest there are big cities as well as small towns and farms on huge, open grasslands. A large area of these grasslands is known as the Great Plains.

Coyotes, gophers, and prairie dogs live on the plains.

There are enormous dairy farms, cattle ranches, and farms growing wheat, corn, and other grains.

The Great Lakes

Canada

Lake Superior

Sault Sainte Marie

Lake Huron

The Great Lakes are five very large lakes along the northern edge of the Midwest.

Lake Michigan

Toronto

Lake Ontario

Hamilton
Niagara Falls
Buffalo

Port Huron

Milwaukee

Detroit

Lake Erie

Chicago

United States

Cleveland

The first skyscrapers were built in Chicago, Illinois.

Ships cross the Great Lakes to the Atlantic Ocean carrying goods and farm produce from the Midwest all over the world.

In St Louis, Missouri, a huge steel arch was built to honor the city's role as "Gateway to the West" for wagon trains in the nineteenth century.

Steel, rubber, and cars are produced in the cities of the Midwest.

The West

In the West – the country's biggest region – there are mountains, forests, and deserts. The region gets its wealth from mining, crop and cattle farming, forestry, high technology, and tourism.

Yellowstone, in Wyoming, was the country's first national park.

People go to the national parks to see grizzly bears, wolves, mountain lions, deer, and moose.

"Silicon Valley" in California is where all kinds of electronic equipment are made, including parts for satellites and computers.

Rattlesnakes live in the West. The "rattle" is in their tail and can be heard from far away.

Cactus plants are found in the deserts. Some can grow 50 feet (15 meters) high.

The beautiful Golden Gate Bridge is suspended across the entrance to San Francisco Bay.

Tourists come from all over the world to see the faces of four presidents carved on Mount Rushmore, South Dakota.

You can feel the bridge sway as you walk across it.

North America

North America contains Canada, the United States of America, Mexico, and the countries of Central America. Canada is the second largest country in the world. The U.S. is the fourth largest and has fifty states.

The Canadian flag

Ice hockey is a very popular sport in Canada.

Skiing is popular in the Rocky mountains. The Rockies run from Canada, through the United States.

Canadian police are called Mounties. Some still ride horses, but most drive cars or motorcycles nowadays.

The U.S. produces more timber than any other country.

Alaska (USA)

Yukon River
Alaskan Mountains
Fairbanks •
• Anchorage

Great Bear Lake
Mackenzie River
Great Slave Lake

Lake Athabasca

Rocky Mountains

Columbia River
Snake River

Vancouver

Fact file

Highest mountain: Mount McKinley, Alaska, 20,322 ft (6,194 m).

Longest River: Mississippi-Missouri River, U.S., 3,860 miles (6,212 km).

Largest Lake: Lake Superior, U.S.-Canada, is the second largest in the world. 31,800 sq. miles (82,383 sq km).

Weather: Canada and Alaska are colder than the rest of North America.

Biggest City: Mexico City, Mexico, about 9 million people.

Number of people: Canada, about 30 million. U.S., about 256 million. Mexico, about 86 million. Costa Rica, about 3 million. Panama, about 3 million.

One of the world's most active volcanos, Mauna Loa, is in Hawaii.

Hawaii (USA)

The Aztecs were a civilization in Mexico hundreds of years ago. Mexicans are proud of their Aztec ancestry.

Coastal Mountains
Sierra Nevada
Colorado River

Los Angeles •
San Diego •

The American flag

Pacific Ocean

Bananas, coffee, and sugar are grown in Central America.

The Mexican flag

KM	250	500	1000	1500	2000	2500	3000	3500	4000	4500	5000	5500	6000	6500
MILES		250	500	1000		1500	2000		2500		3000		3500		4000

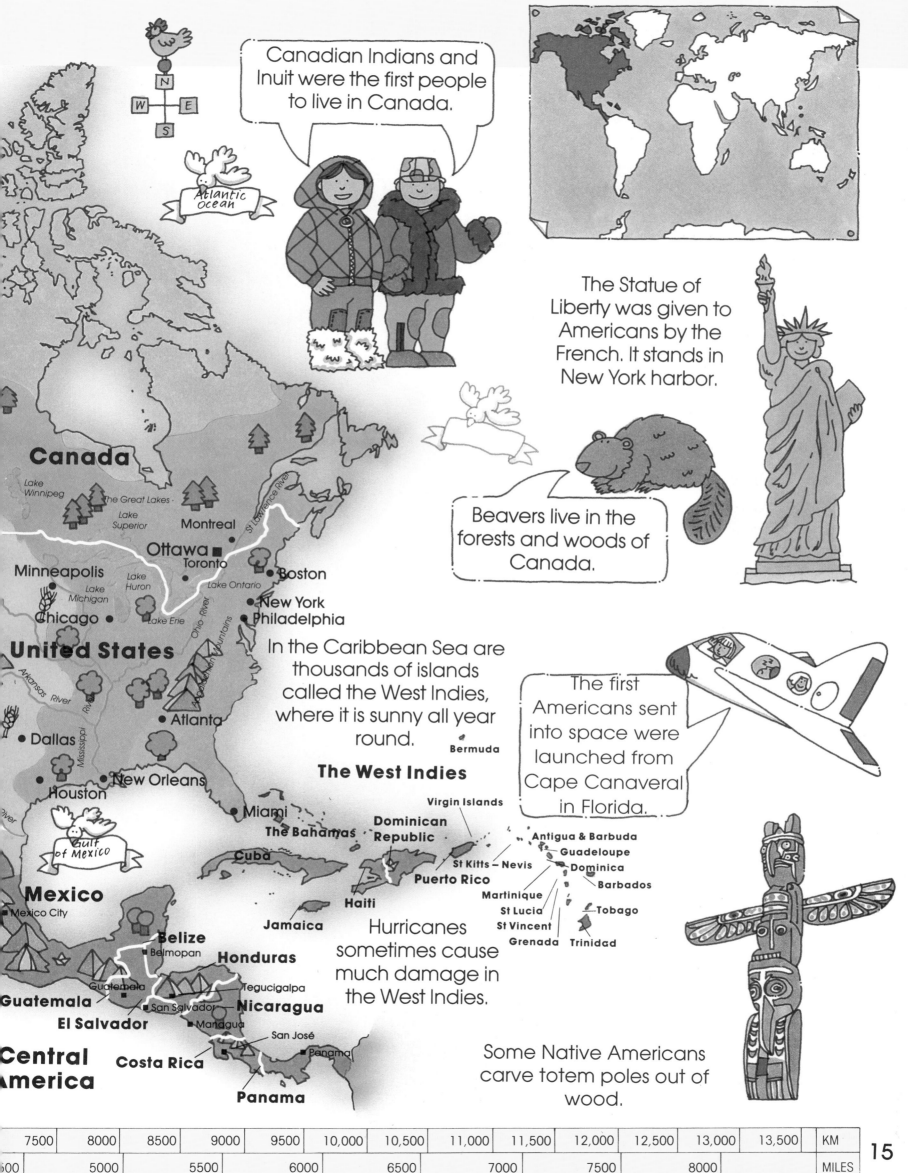

Canadian Indians and Inuit were the first people to live in Canada.

Atlantic ocean

The Statue of Liberty was given to Americans by the French. It stands in New York harbor.

Beavers live in the forests and woods of Canada.

Canada

Lake Winnipeg
The Great Lakes
Lake Superior
Montreal
St Lawrence River
Lake Michigan
Lake Huron
Ottawa Toronto
Minneapolis
Lake Ontario
Lake Erie
Boston
Chicago
Ohio River
New York
Philadelphia
United States
Arkansas River
Appalachian Mountains
Atlanta
Dallas
Mississippi River
New Orleans
Houston
Gulf of Mexico
Miami

In the Caribbean Sea are thousands of islands called the West Indies, where it is sunny all year round.

Bermuda

The West Indies

Virgin Islands

The first Americans sent into space were launched from Cape Canaveral in Florida.

The Bahamas
Dominican Republic
St Kitts – Nevis
Puerto Rico
Antigua & Barbuda
Guadeloupe
Dominica
Barbados
Martinique
St Lucia
Tobago
St Vincent
Grenada Trinidad

Cuba
Mexico
Mexico City
Haiti
Jamaica

Belize
Belmopan
Honduras
Guatemala
Tegucigalpa
Guatemala
San Salvador
Nicaragua
El Salvador
Managua
San José
Panama
Central America
Costa Rica
Panama

Hurricanes sometimes cause much damage in the West Indies.

Some Native Americans carve totem poles out of wood.

	7500	8000	8500	9000	9500	10,000	10,500	11,000	11,500	12,000	12,500	13,000	13,500	KM
500		5000		5500		6000		6500		7000		7500		8000		MILES

South America

South America is the fourth largest continent. It is made up of 13 different countries. There are mountains and rain forests as well as plains and deserts. The weather ranges from very hot to very cold.

The Brazilian flag

Hummingbirds are found in rain forests. They are very tiny and brightly colored.

Anteaters also live in the rain forests. They use their long, sticky tongues to eat ants.

Rubber trees grow in South America. The tree bark is cut and the sticky sap runs out. It is collected to make rubber products.

Llamas are used to carry things in the Andes. Their thick fur protects them from the cold.

The Chilean flag

The Ecuadorean flag

Copper mines in northern Chile supply the world with copper.

Galapagos Islands

Ecuador

Caracus
Angel Falls
Venezuela
Orinoco River
Guyana
Suriname
French Guiana
Georgetown
Bogota
Guiana Highlands
Paramaribo
Cayenne
Colombia
Quito
Amazon River
Manaos
Peru
Lima
Bolivia
La Paz
Paraguay River
Parana River
Brasilia
Paraguay
Asuncion
Chile
Andes Mountains
Santiago
Uruguay
Buenos Aires
Montevideo
Argentina
Falkland Islands

KM	250	500	1000	1500	2000	2500	3000	3500	4000	4500	5000	5500
MILES		250	500	1000		1500	2000	2500		3000		3500

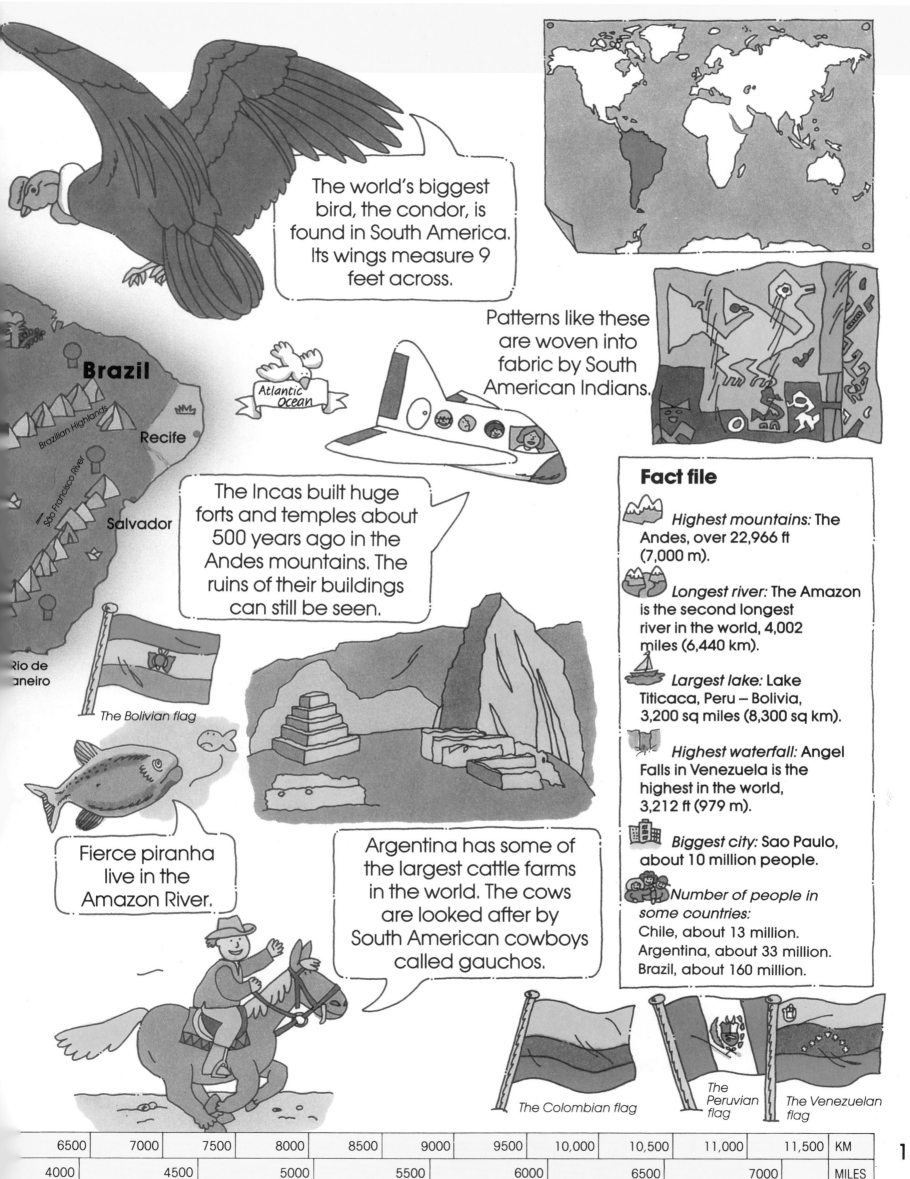

The world's biggest bird, the condor, is found in South America. Its wings measure 9 feet across.

Patterns like these are woven into fabric by South American Indians.

Atlantic Ocean

Brazil

Brazilian Highlands

Recife

São Francisco River

Salvador

Rio de Janeiro

The Incas built huge forts and temples about 500 years ago in the Andes mountains. The ruins of their buildings can still be seen.

The Bolivian flag

Fierce piranha live in the Amazon River.

Argentina has some of the largest cattle farms in the world. The cows are looked after by South American cowboys called gauchos.

Fact file

Highest mountains: The Andes, over 22,966 ft (7,000 m).

Longest river: The Amazon is the second longest river in the world, 4,002 miles (6,440 km).

Largest lake: Lake Titicaca, Peru – Bolivia, 3,200 sq miles (8,300 sq km).

Highest waterfall: Angel Falls in Venezuela is the highest in the world, 3,212 ft (979 m).

Biggest city: Sao Paulo, about 10 million people.

Number of people in some countries:
Chile, about 13 million.
Argentina, about 33 million.
Brazil, about 160 million.

The Colombian flag

The Peruvian flag

The Venezuelan flag

6500	7000	7500	8000	8500	9000	9500	10,000	10,500	11,000	11,500	KM
4000		4500		5000		5500		6000		6500		7000		MILES

Northern Europe

These northern European countries are known as Scandinavia. Norway has over 150,000 islands along its coastline. The Norwegian coast is jagged, with deep inlets called fjords. Forests and lakes cover large areas of Scandinavia. Many bears and wolves used to live in the forests.

Workers travel to the oil rigs by helicopter.

Children here learn to ski almost as soon as they can walk!

There is oil under the sea bed. Oil rigs are used to pump the oil up to the surface.

The oil is used as fuel for cars and for heating buildings.

Norwegian Sea

North Sea

Trawlers are fishing boats that catch fish by dragging nets along the sea bed. Many Norwegian fishing boats fish in the North Sea.

Some fishing boats can stay out at sea for months at a time.

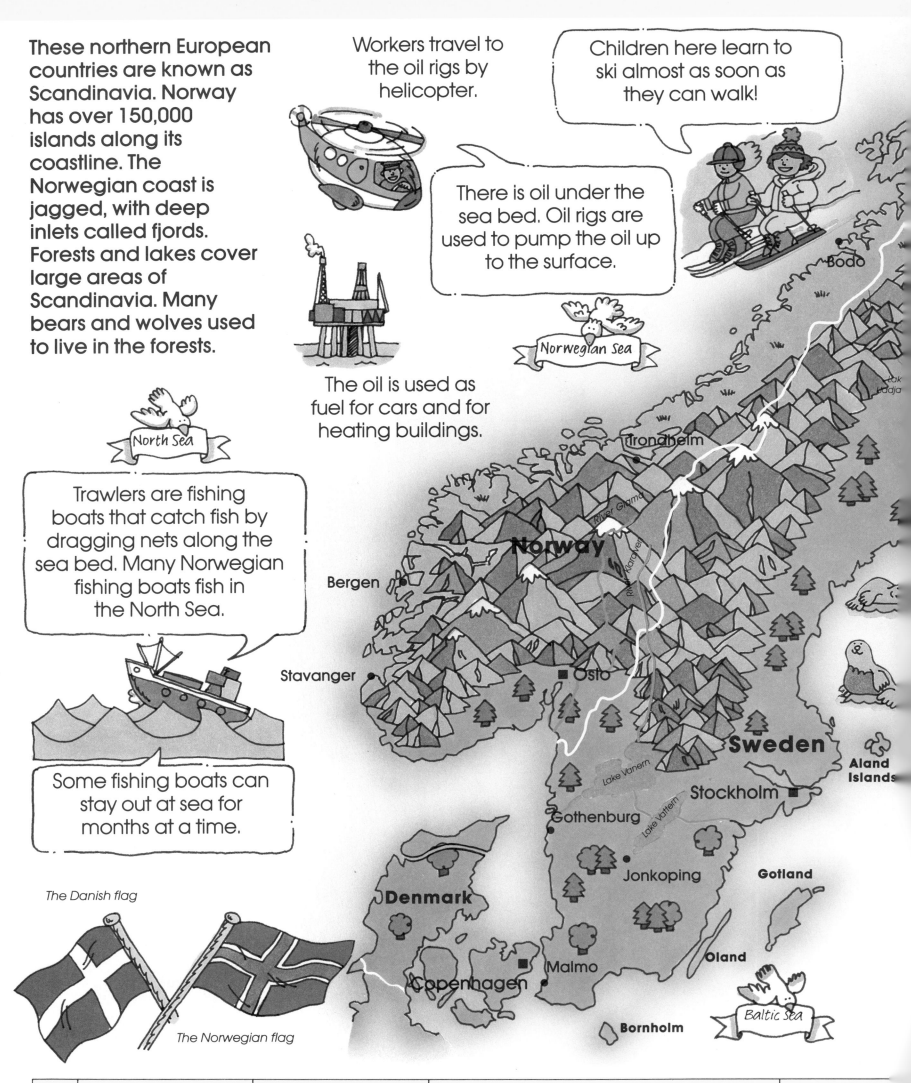

Bodo

Lak Uddja

Trondheim

River Glama

Norway

River Klaralven

Bergen

Stavanger

Oslo

Sweden

Aland Islands

Lake Vanern

Stockholm

Gothenburg

Lake Vattern

Jonkoping

Gotland

Denmark

Oland

The Danish flag

Malmo

Copenhagen

Bornholm

Baltic Sea

The Norwegian flag

	KM		250		500		1000	
	MILES			250		500		

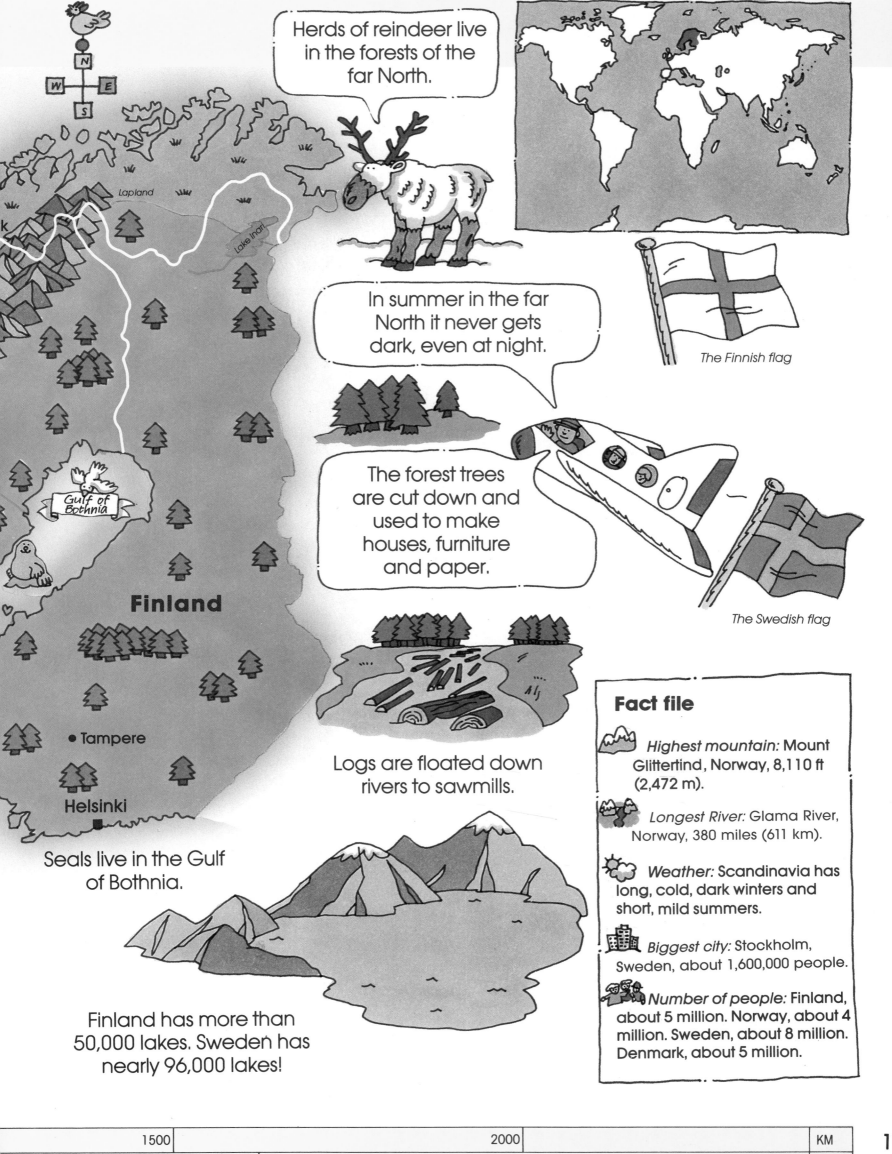

Herds of reindeer live in the forests of the far North.

In summer in the far North it never gets dark, even at night.

The forest trees are cut down and used to make houses, furniture and paper.

Logs are floated down rivers to sawmills.

Lapland

Lake Inari

k

Gulf of Bothnia

Finland

• Tampere

Helsinki

Seals live in the Gulf of Bothnia.

Finland has more than 50,000 lakes. Sweden has nearly 96,000 lakes!

The Finnish flag

The Swedish flag

Fact file

Highest mountain: Mount Glittertind, Norway, 8,110 ft (2,472 m).

Longest River: Glama River, Norway, 380 miles (611 km).

Weather: Scandinavia has long, cold, dark winters and short, mild summers.

Biggest city: Stockholm, Sweden, about 1,600,000 people.

Number of people: Finland, about 5 million. Norway, about 4 million. Sweden, about 8 million. Denmark, about 5 million.

| | 1500 | | 2000 | | KM |
| | | 1000 | | | MILES |

Britain and Central Europe

On this map you can see seventeen different countries. Some, like Luxembourg, are tiny. Others, such as France, are large. There are very high mountains, called the Alps, in Switzerland, France, and Austria, but most of the rest of Europe is flatter. The flat land is very good for farming.

Northern Ireland

Ireland is known as the Emerald Isle because of its beautiful green hills and fields.

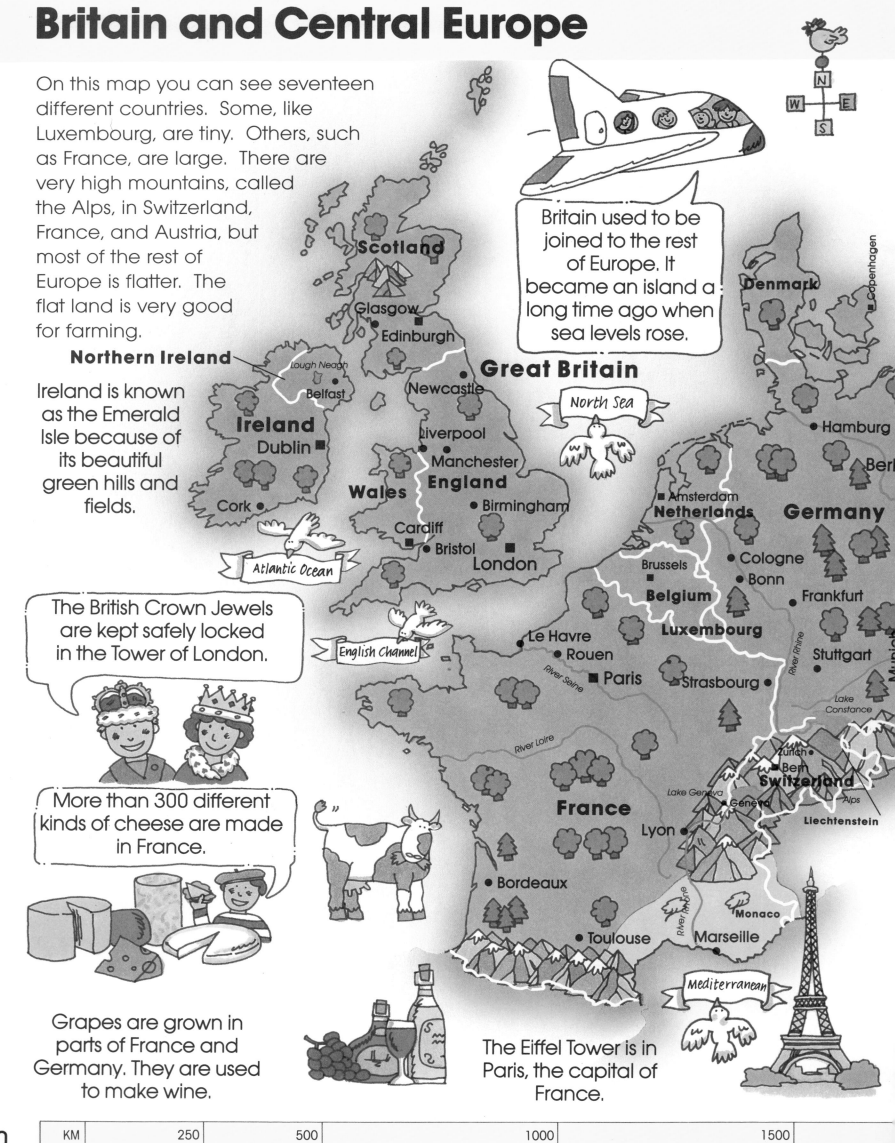

Britain used to be joined to the rest of Europe. It became an island a long time ago when sea levels rose.

The British Crown Jewels are kept safely locked in the Tower of London.

More than 300 different kinds of cheese are made in France.

Grapes are grown in parts of France and Germany. They are used to make wine.

The Eiffel Tower is in Paris, the capital of France.

Scotland
Glasgow
Edinburgh
Lough Neagh
Belfast
Ireland
Dublin
Cork
Wales
Cardiff
Bristol
Newcastle
Great Britain
Liverpool
Manchester
England
Birmingham
London
North Sea
Atlantic Ocean
English Channel
Le Havre
Rouen
Paris
River Seine
River Loire
Bordeaux
France
Toulouse
Lyon
Denmark
Copenhagen
Hamburg
Amsterdam
Netherlands
Brussels
Belgium
Luxembourg
Germany
Cologne
Bonn
Frankfurt
Stuttgart
River Rhine
Strasbourg
Lake Constance
Zurich
Bern
Switzerland
Lake Geneva
Geneva
Alps
Liechtenstein
River Rhône
Monaco
Marseille
Mediterranean

	KM	250	500		1000		1500	
	MILES		250		500			1000

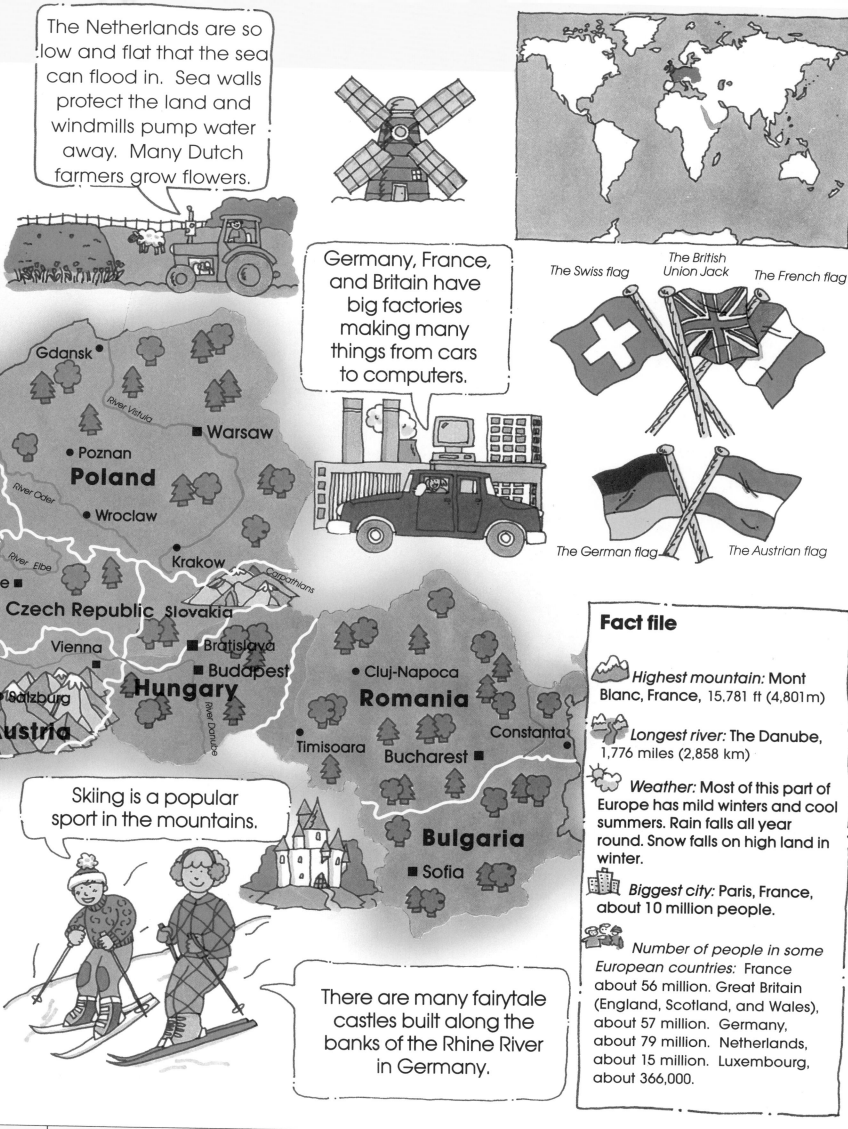

The Netherlands are so low and flat that the sea can flood in. Sea walls protect the land and windmills pump water away. Many Dutch farmers grow flowers.

The Swiss flag

The British Union Jack

The French flag

Germany, France, and Britain have big factories making many things from cars to computers.

The German flag

The Austrian flag

Gdansk

River Vistula

Warsaw

Poznan

Poland

River Oder

Wroclaw

River Elbe

Krakow

Carpathians

gue

Czech Republic Slovakia

Vienna

Bratislava

Budapest

Salzburg

Hungary

River Danube

Austria

Cluj-Napoca

Romania

Timisoara

Constanta

Bucharest

Bulgaria

Sofia

Skiing is a popular sport in the mountains.

There are many fairytale castles built along the banks of the Rhine River in Germany.

Fact file

Highest mountain: Mont Blanc, France, 15,781 ft (4,801m)

Longest river: The Danube, 1,776 miles (2,858 km)

Weather: Most of this part of Europe has mild winters and cool summers. Rain falls all year round. Snow falls on high land in winter.

Biggest city: Paris, France, about 10 million people.

Number of people in some European countries: France about 56 million. Great Britain (England, Scotland, and Wales), about 57 million. Germany, about 79 million. Netherlands, about 15 million. Luxembourg, about 366,000.

| 2000 | | 2500 | | 3000 | | 3500 | KM |
| 1500 | | | | 2000 | | | MILES |

Mediterranean Europe

The countries around the Mediterranean Sea are sunny all year. Olives, fruit, and vegetables are grown in all these countries. Many people go to the Mediterranean for vacations. In parts of Spain and Italy there are high mountains where people ski in the winter.

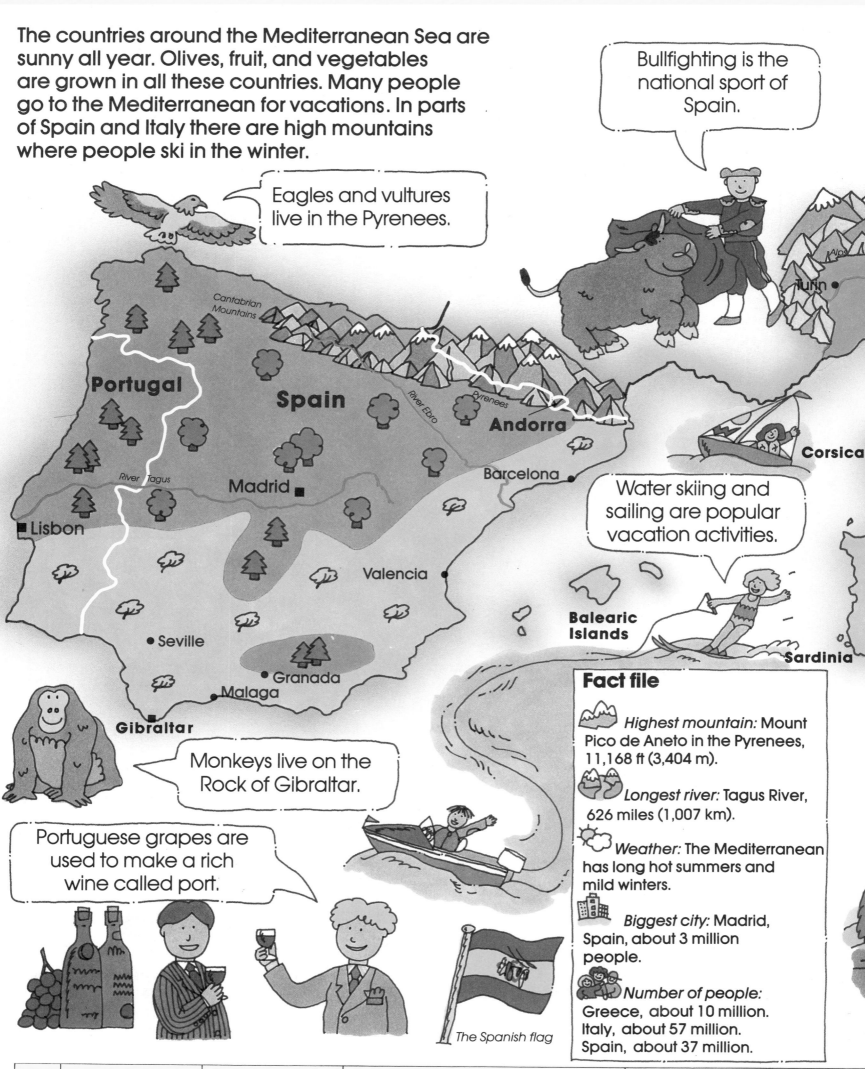

Bullfighting is the national sport of Spain.

Eagles and vultures live in the Pyrenees.

Water skiing and sailing are popular vacation activities.

Monkeys live on the Rock of Gibraltar.

Portuguese grapes are used to make a rich wine called port.

The Spanish flag

Fact file

Highest mountain: Mount Pico de Aneto in the Pyrenees, 11,168 ft (3,404 m).

Longest river: Tagus River, 626 miles (1,007 km).

Weather: The Mediterranean has long hot summers and mild winters.

Biggest city: Madrid, Spain, about 3 million people.

Number of people: Greece, about 10 million. Italy, about 57 million. Spain, about 37 million.

| KM | | 250 | | 500 | | | 1000 |
| MILES | | | 250 | | | 500 | |

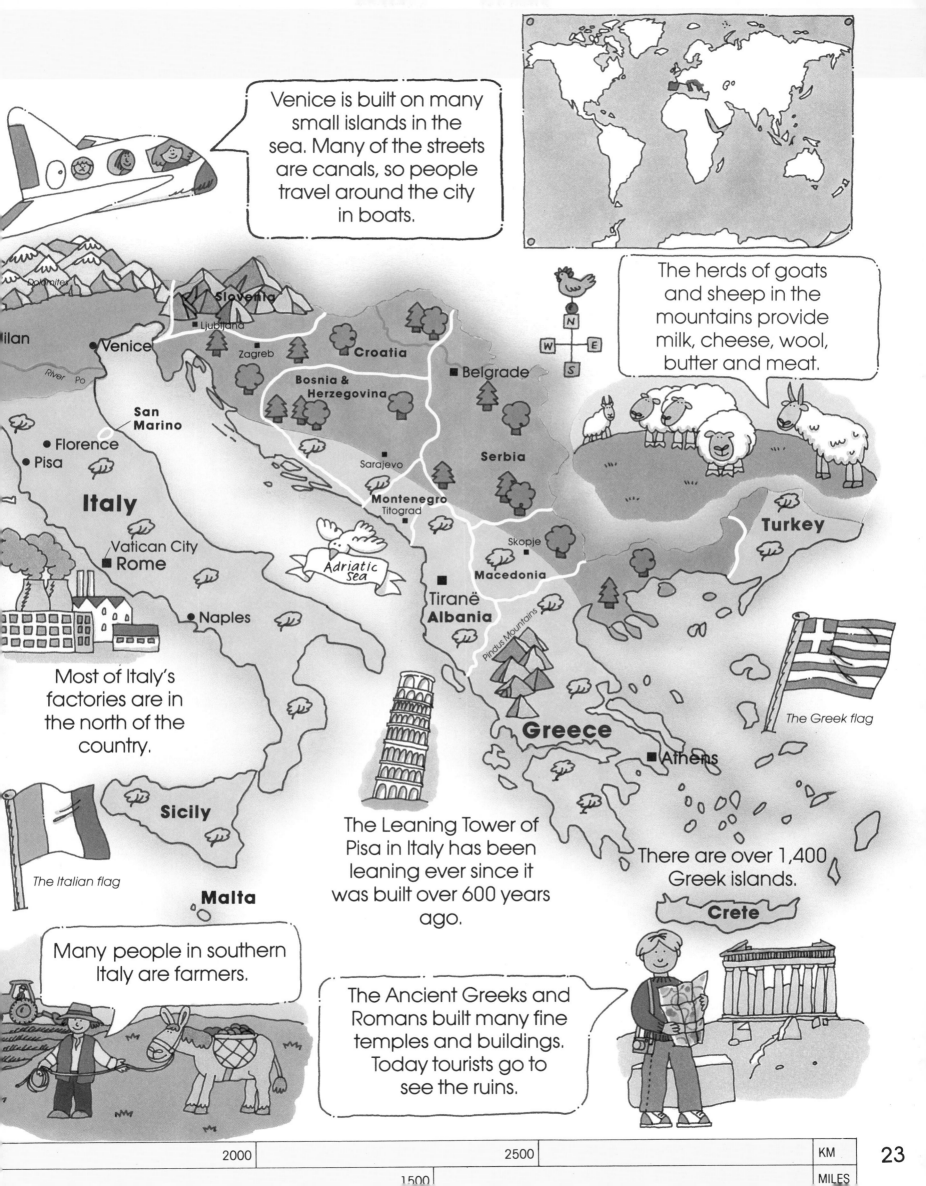

Venice is built on many small islands in the sea. Many of the streets are canals, so people travel around the city in boats.

The herds of goats and sheep in the mountains provide milk, cheese, wool, butter and meat.

Dolomites

Slovenia

Ljubljana

Milan

Venice

Zagreb

Croatia

River Po

Bosnia & Herzegovina

Belgrade

San Marino

Florence

Pisa

Sarajevo

Serbia

Italy

Montenegro
Titograd

Vatican City

Rome

Adriatic Sea

Skopje

Naples

Macedonia

Turkey

Tiranë

Albania

Pindus Mountains

Greece

The Greek flag

Most of Italy's factories are in the north of the country.

Athens

The Leaning Tower of Pisa in Italy has been leaning ever since it was built over 600 years ago.

There are over 1,400 Greek islands.

Sicily

Crete

The Italian flag

Malta

Many people in southern Italy are farmers.

The Ancient Greeks and Romans built many fine temples and buildings. Today tourists go to see the ruins.

| 2000 | 2500 | KM |
| 1500 | | MILES |

Africa

Africa is the second largest continent in the world. It is split up into lots of different countries. Most of Africa is covered in grassland and desert. Some of the tropical rain forests in Africa have been chopped down to build villages and farms.

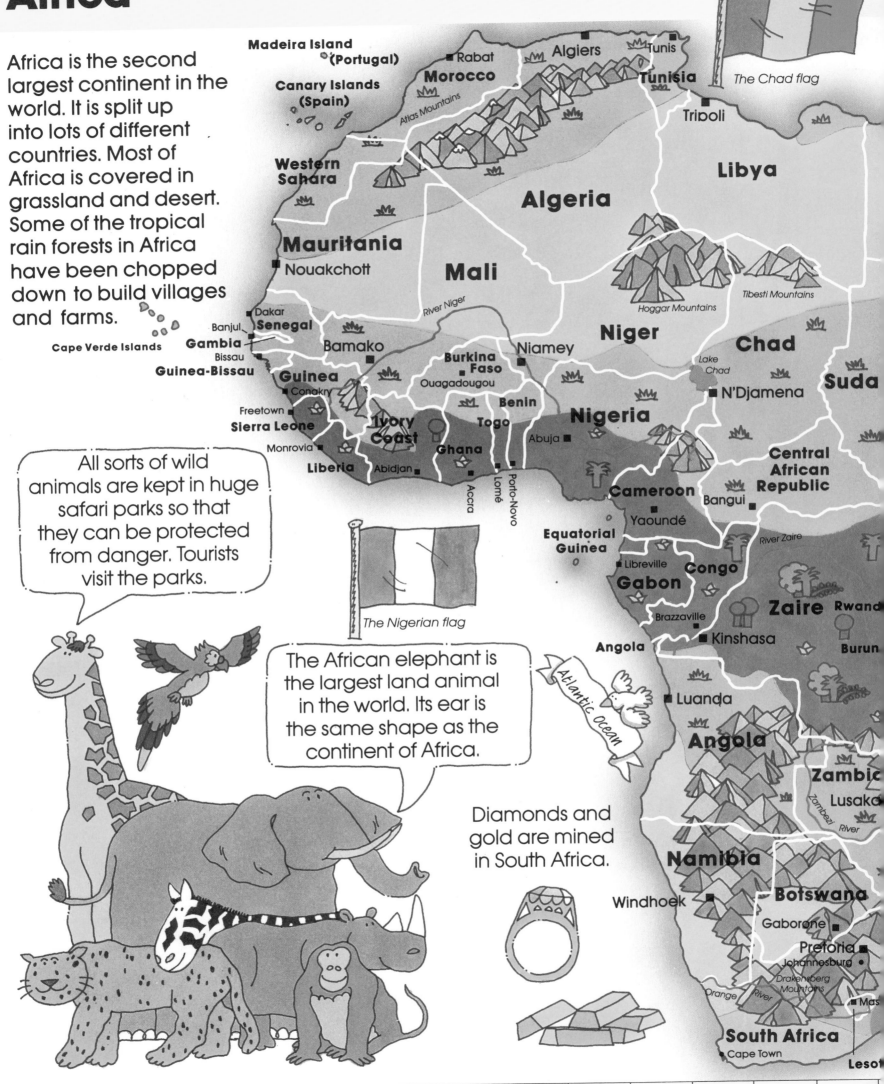

Madeira Island (Portugal)

Canary Islands (Spain)

Cape Verde Islands

The Chad flag

Rabat
Morocco
Atlas Mountains
Western Sahara
Mauritania
Nouakchott
Dakar
Banjul Senegal
Gambia
Bissau
Guinea-Bissau
Guinea
Conakry
Freetown
Sierra Leone
Monrovia
Liberia
Ivory Coast
Abidjan
Accra

Algiers
Tunis
Tunisia
Tripoli
Libya
Algeria
Hoggar Mountains
Tibesti Mountains
Mali
River Niger
Niger
Chad
Lake Chad
Niamey
N'Djamena
Suda
Bamako
Burkina Faso
Ouagadougou
Benin
Togo
Nigeria
Ghana
Abuja
Lomé
Porto-Novo
Cameroon
Yaoundé
Bangui
Central African Republic
Equatorial Guinea
Libreville
Gabon
Congo
Brazzaville
Kinshasa
Zaire
Rwand
Burun
Angola
River Zaire

All sorts of wild animals are kept in huge safari parks so that they can be protected from danger. Tourists visit the parks.

The Nigerian flag

The African elephant is the largest land animal in the world. Its ear is the same shape as the continent of Africa.

Atlantic Ocean

Luanda
Angola
Zambic
Lusaka
Zambezi River

Diamonds and gold are mined in South Africa.

Namibia

Botswana

Windhoek
Gaborone
Pretoria
Johannesburg
Drakensberg Mountains
Orange River
Mas

South Africa
Cape Town
Leso

24

KM	250	500		1000	1500	2000	2500	3000	3500	4000	4500	5000	5500	6000	6500
MILES		250	500		1000		1500		2000		2500		3000		3500	4000

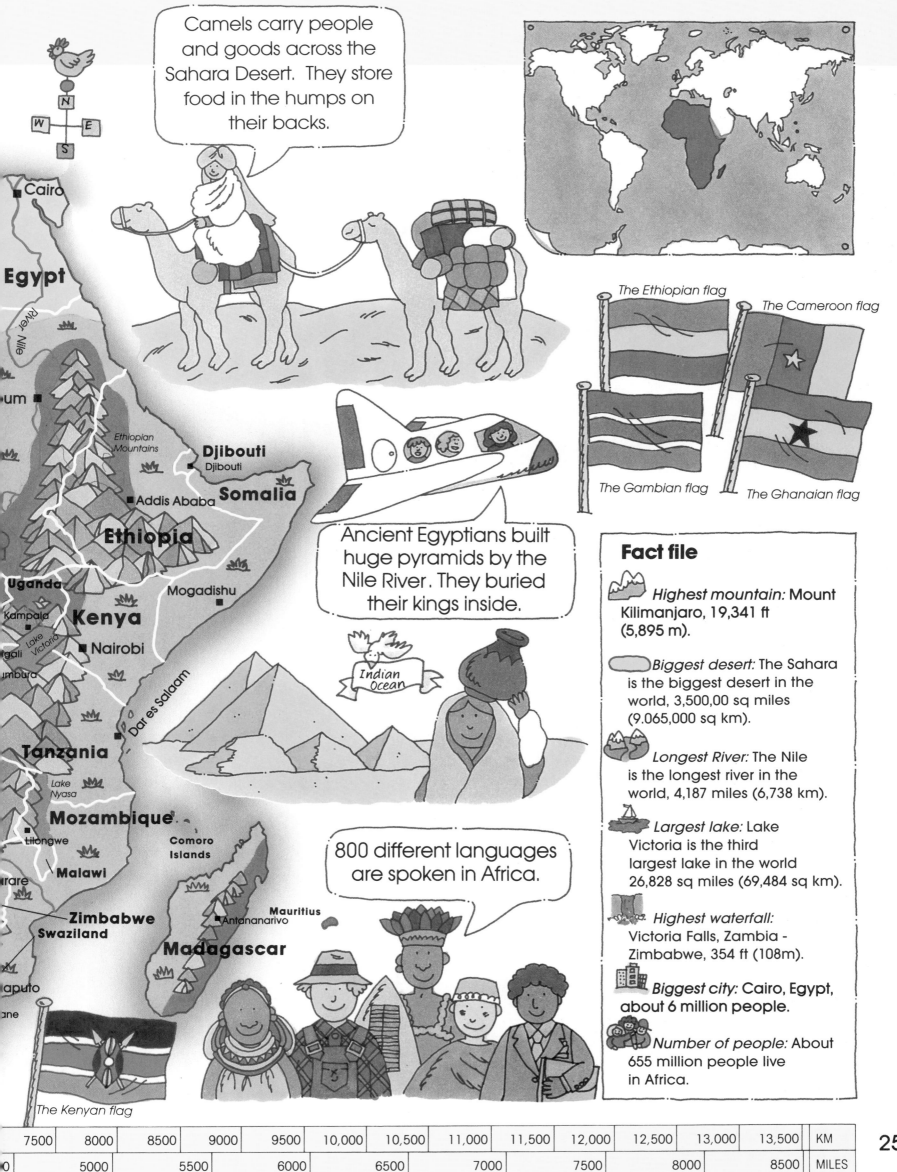

Camels carry people and goods across the Sahara Desert. They store food in the humps on their backs.

Egypt

Cairo

River Nile

um

Ethiopian Mountains

Djibouti
Djibouti

Somalia

Addis Ababa

Ethiopia

Uganda

Mogadishu

Kampala

Kenya

gali

Lake Victoria

Nairobi

mbura

Dar es Salaam

Tanzania

Lake Nyasa

Mozambique

Lilongwe

Comoro Islands

Malawi

rare

Zimbabwe

Swaziland

Mauritius
Antananarivo

Madagascar

aputo

ane

The Kenyan flag

The Ethiopian flag

The Cameroon flag

The Gambian flag

The Ghanaian flag

Ancient Egyptians built huge pyramids by the Nile River. They buried their kings inside.

Indian Ocean

800 different languages are spoken in Africa.

Fact file

Highest mountain: Mount Kilimanjaro, 19,341 ft (5,895 m).

Biggest desert: The Sahara is the biggest desert in the world, 3,500,00 sq miles (9.065,000 sq km).

Longest River: The Nile is the longest river in the world, 4,187 miles (6,738 km).

Largest lake: Lake Victoria is the third largest lake in the world 26,828 sq miles (69,484 sq km).

Highest waterfall: Victoria Falls, Zambia - Zimbabwe, 354 ft (108m).

Biggest city: Cairo, Egypt, about 6 million people.

Number of people: About 655 million people live in Africa.

	7500	8000	8500	9000	9500	10,000	10,500	11,000	11,500	12,000	12,500	13,000	13,500	KM
0		5000		5500		6000		6500		7000		7500		8000	8500	MILES

The Former U.S.S.R.

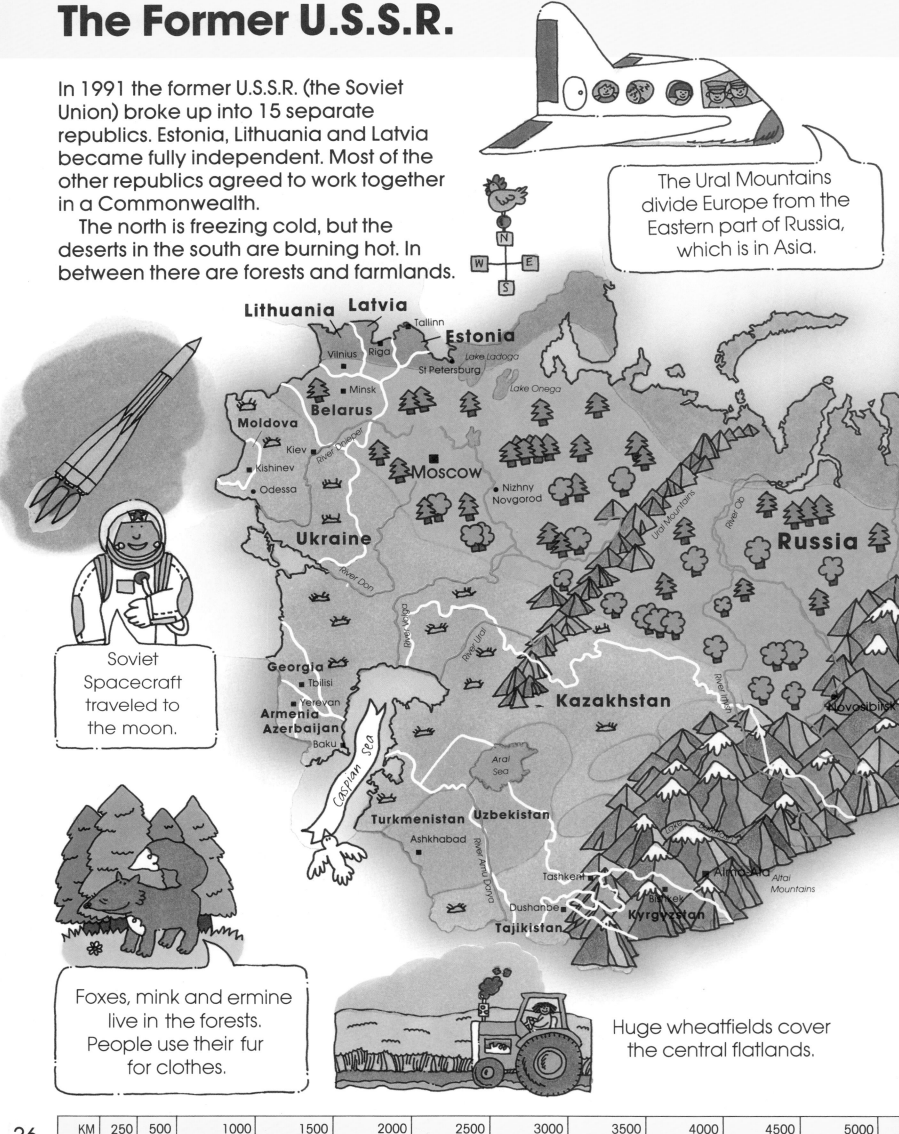

In 1991 the former U.S.S.R. (the Soviet Union) broke up into 15 separate republics. Estonia, Lithuania and Latvia became fully independent. Most of the other republics agreed to work together in a Commonwealth.

The north is freezing cold, but the deserts in the south are burning hot. In between there are forests and farmlands.

The Ural Mountains divide Europe from the Eastern part of Russia, which is in Asia.

Soviet Spacecraft traveled to the moon.

Foxes, mink and ermine live in the forests. People use their fur for clothes.

Huge wheatfields cover the central flatlands.

Lithuania
Latvia
Estonia
Vilnius
Riga
Tallinn
St Petersburg
Lake Ladoga
Lake Onega
Minsk
Belarus
Moldova
Kiev
River Dnieper
Kishinev
Odessa
Moscow
Nizhny Novgorod
Ural Mountains
River Ob
River Yenisey
Russia
Ukraine
River Don
River Volga
River Ural
River Irtish
Kazakhstan
Novosibirsk
Georgia
Tbilisi
Yerevan
Armenia
Azerbaijan
Baku
Caspian Sea
Aral Sea
Turkmenistan
Uzbekistan
Ashkhabad
River Amu Darya
Tashkent
Almo-Ata
Altai Mountains
Lake Balkhash
Dushanbe
Bishkek
Kyrgyzstan
Tajikistan

KM	250	500	1000	1500	2000	2500	3000	3500	4000	4500	5000
MILES	250		500		1000		1500		2000		2500		3000	

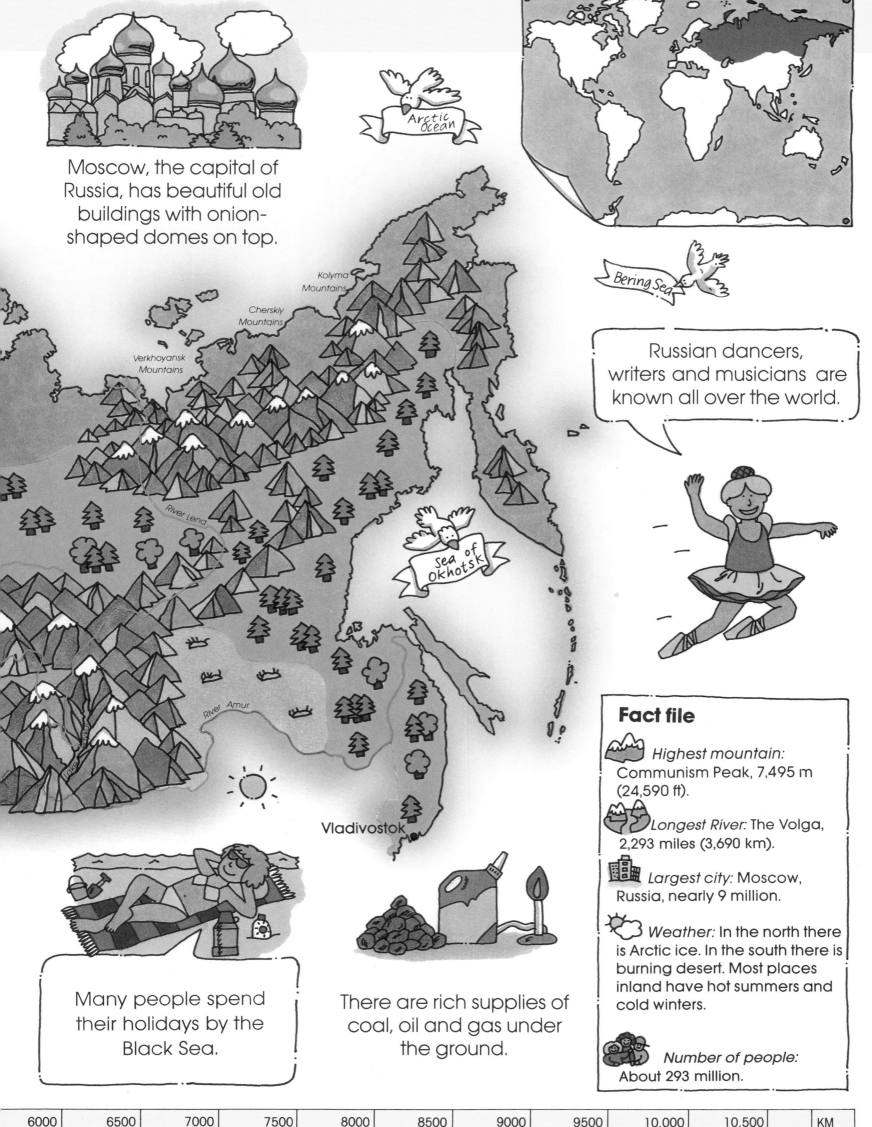

Moscow, the capital of Russia, has beautiful old buildings with onion-shaped domes on top.

Arctic Ocean

Bering Sea

Kolyma Mountains

Cherskiy Mountains

Verkhoyansk Mountains

River Lena

Sea of Okhotsk

River Amur

Vladivostok

Russian dancers, writers and musicians are known all over the world.

Many people spend their holidays by the Black Sea.

There are rich supplies of coal, oil and gas under the ground.

Fact file

Highest mountain: Communism Peak, 7,495 m (24,590 ft).

Longest River: The Volga, 2,293 miles (3,690 km).

Largest city: Moscow, Russia, nearly 9 million.

Weather: In the north there is Arctic ice. In the south there is burning desert. Most places inland have hot summers and cold winters.

Number of people: About 293 million.

6000	6500	7000	7500	8000	8500	9000	9500	10,000	10,500	KM
	4000		4500		5000		5500		6000		6500	MILES

The Middle East

Most of the Middle East is either mountainous or hot, sandy desert. Some of the countries have a great deal of valuable oil under the ground. The oil is pumped up to the surface at oil wells. It is then sold to other countries for use as gasoline and other kinds of fuel.

The Israeli flag

Black Sea

The United Arab Emirates flag

Istanbul · Ankara · Turkey · Taurus Mountains · River Euphrates · River Tigris · Cyprus · Nicosia · Mediterranean Sea · Syria · Lebanon · Beirut · Damascus · Baghdad · Iraq · Israel · Tel Aviv · Jerusalem · Amman · Jordan · Basra · Kuwait City · Kuwait · Bahrain · Al-Manam · Do · Saudi Arabia · Riyadh · Mecca · Red Sea · San'a · Aden

Jerusalem, in Israel, is a holy city for Jews, Christians and Muslims.

Every year millions of Muslims make a special journey to their holy city of Mecca, in Saudi Arabia.

The desert in the south of Saudi Arabia covers almost a quarter of the country. It is the largest stretch of sand in the world.

28

KM		250	500		1000		1500		2000		2500
MILES			250	500			1000			1500	

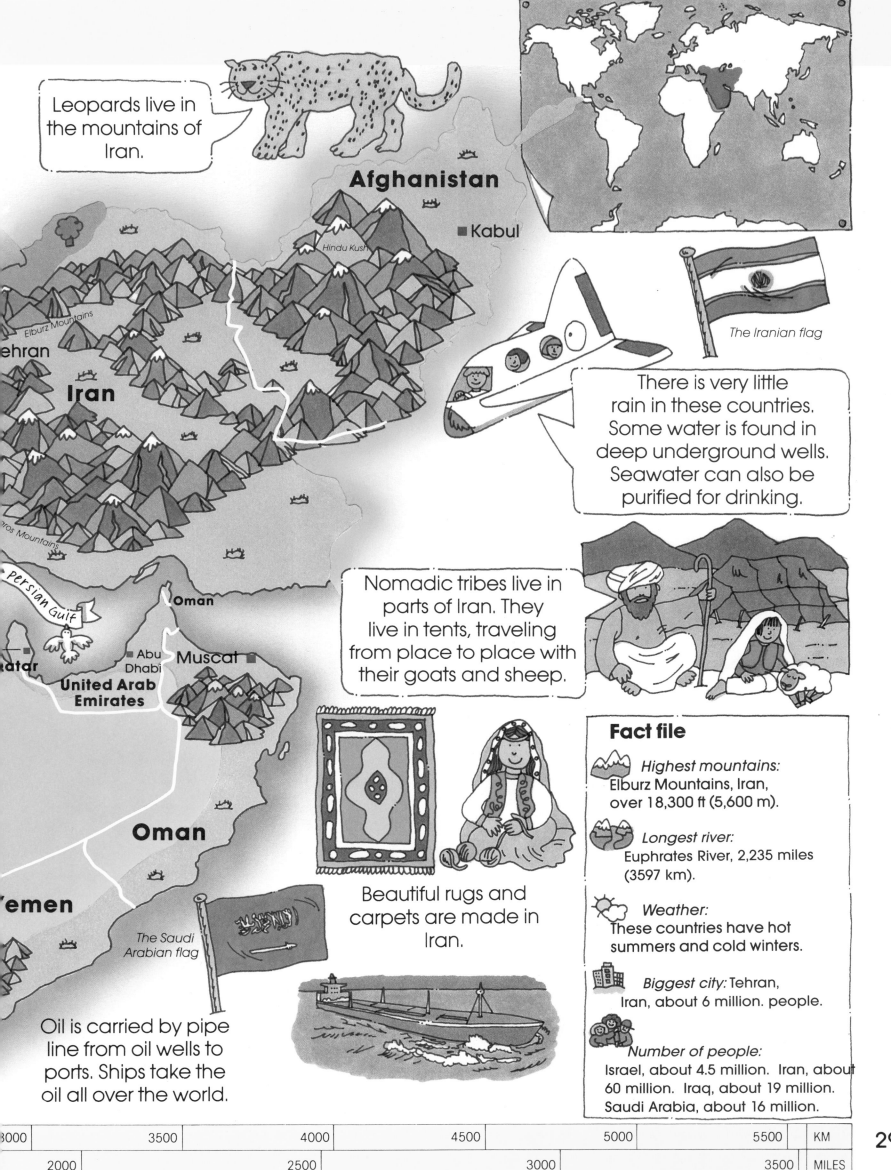

Leopards live in the mountains of Iran.

Afghanistan

■ Kabul

Hindu Kush

Elburz Mountains

ehran

Iran

ros Mountains

Persian Gulf

Oman

■ Abu Dhabi

Muscat ■

aatar

United Arab Emirates

Oman

'emen

The Saudi Arabian flag

The Iranian flag

There is very little rain in these countries. Some water is found in deep underground wells. Seawater can also be purified for drinking.

Nomadic tribes live in parts of Iran. They live in tents, traveling from place to place with their goats and sheep.

Beautiful rugs and carpets are made in Iran.

Oil is carried by pipe line from oil wells to ports. Ships take the oil all over the world.

Fact file

Highest mountains: Elburz Mountains, Iran, over 18,300 ft (5,600 m).

Longest river: Euphrates River, 2,235 miles (3597 km).

Weather: These countries have hot summers and cold winters.

Biggest city: Tehran, Iran, about 6 million. people.

Number of people: Israel, about 4.5 million. Iran, about 60 million. Iraq, about 19 million. Saudi Arabia, about 16 million.

3000	3500	4000	4500	5000	5500	KM
2000		2500		3000	3500	MILES

South Asia

Much of South Asia is farmland, and relies on the heavy monsoon rains between June and October for crops to grow. The Himalayas are the highest mountain range in the world and divide South Asia from China.

The monsoon rains and storms cause terrible floods, which can destroy whole villages.

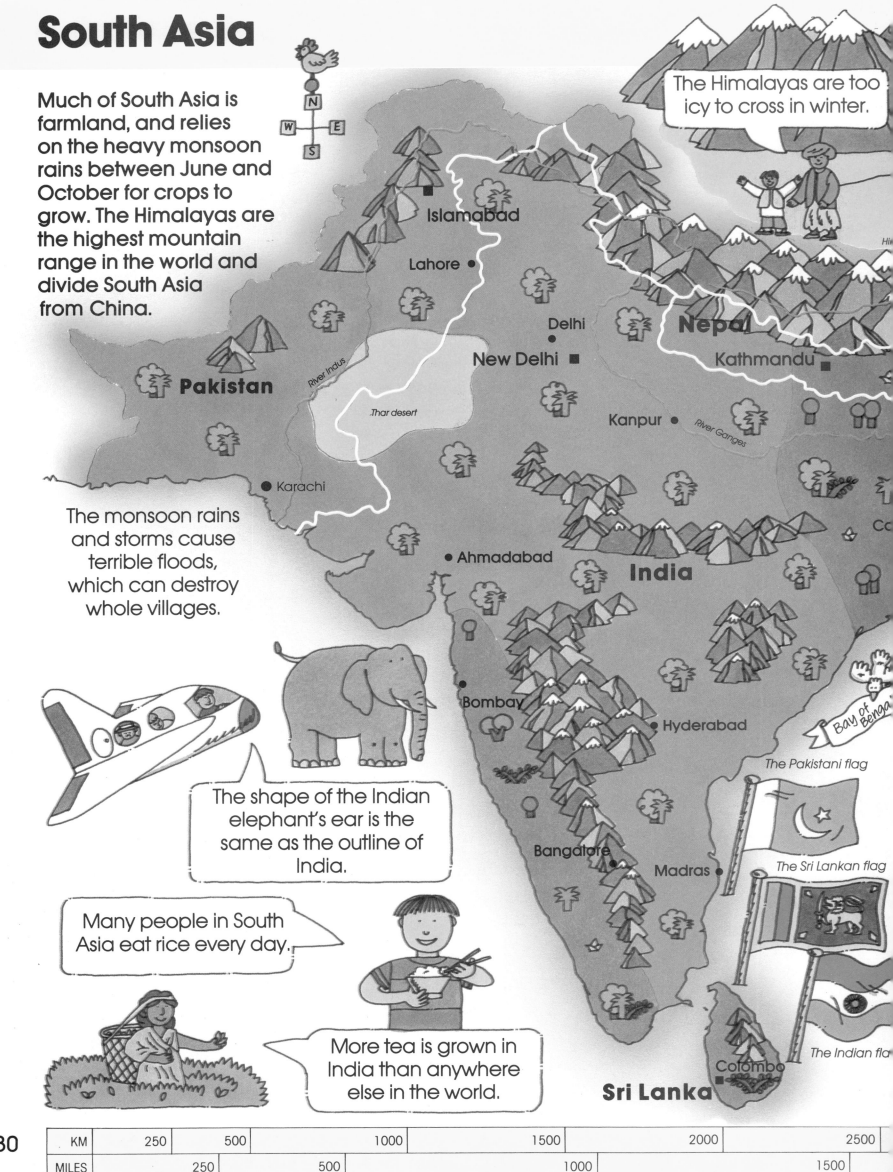

The Himalayas are too icy to cross in winter.

The shape of the Indian elephant's ear is the same as the outline of India.

Many people in South Asia eat rice every day.

More tea is grown in India than anywhere else in the world.

Islamabad

Lahore

Delhi

New Delhi

Nepal

Kathmandu

River Indus

Pakistan

Thar desert

Karachi

Kanpur

River Ganges

Ahmadabad

India

Bombay

Hyderabad

Bay of Bengal

The Pakistani flag

Bangalore

Madras

The Sri Lankan flag

The Indian fla

Colombo

Sri Lanka

	KM	250	500		1000	1500		2000		2500
	MILES		250	500		1000			1500	

Ponies and yaks are used to carry goods across the Himalayas.

Thimbu
Bhutan
River Brahmaputra

Bangladesh

Dhaka

Elephants and tigers live on the lower slopes of the Himalayas and in the swamps of the Ganges River.

India is the second most populous country in the world.

Fact file

Highest mountain: Mount Everest, 29,029 ft (8,848 m).

Longest river: Ganges-Brahmaputra, 1,802 miles (2,900 km).

Weather: It is very cold in the mountains, but hot most of the year elsewhere.

Biggest city: Calcutta, India, about 11 million people.

Number of people in some countries:
Nepal, about 19 million.
Bangledesh, about 180 million.
Bhutan, about 600,000.
India, about 844 million.
Sri Lanka, about 17 million.
Pakistan, about 114 million.

Cows are sacred animals in India. They are not kept in fields but are allowed to graze where they like.

Cotton plants produce threads that are made into cotton fabric. It can be painted or dyed and made into clothes.

The Taj Mahal, near Agra in northern India, is often called the most beautiful building in the world.

| 3000 | | 3500 | | 4000 | | 4500 | | 5000 | | KM |
| | 2000 | | | 2500 | | | 3000 | | | MILES |

Southeast Asia

Southeast Asia is an area that curves from Myanmar through a chain of islands towards Australia. It is warm all the year round, but the monsoon wind brings heavy rains. They can damage the traditional houses made of woven palm leaves.

In Thailand, elephants are used to haul trees from the forest to the river, where they float down to the sawmills.

The Thai flag

Coral are sea creatures that live in the warm, shallow waters of the Pacific. When they die, their hard skeletons form islands and reefs. Millions of coral are needed to make one small island.

Coral islands when seen from above have a turquoise band of sea around them.

Fishing is a way of life for many islanders. Their boats are like canoes with small sails.

Irrawaddy River

Mandalay

Burma

Rangoon

Hanoi

Laos

Vientiane

Vietnam

Thailand

Bangkok

Cambodia

Phnom Penh

South China Sea

Ho Chi Minh City

Brunei

Kuala Lumpur

Medan

Malaysia

Bandar Seri Begawan

Singapore

Jakarta

Indonesia

Semarang

Surabaya

Bandung

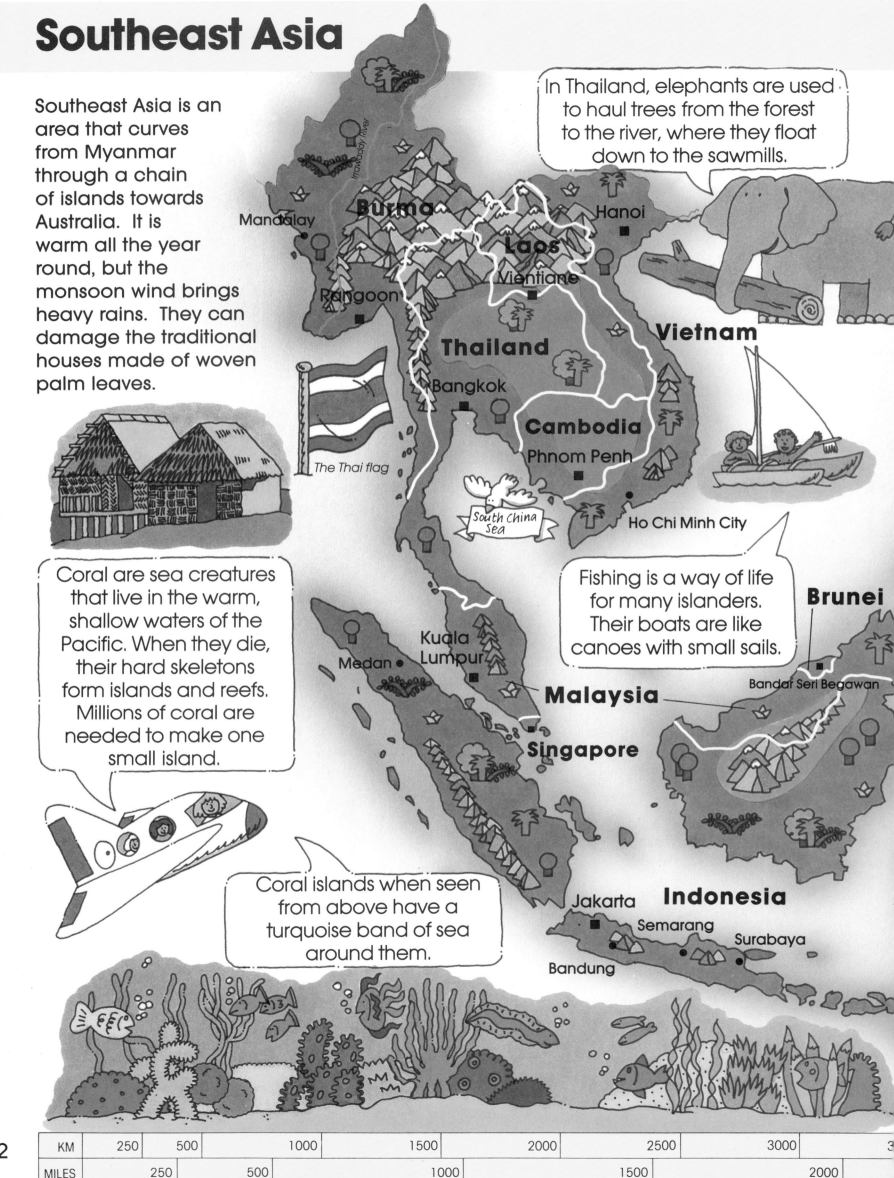

	KM	250	500	1000	1500	2000	2500	3000	3
	MILES		250	500	1000		1500		2000

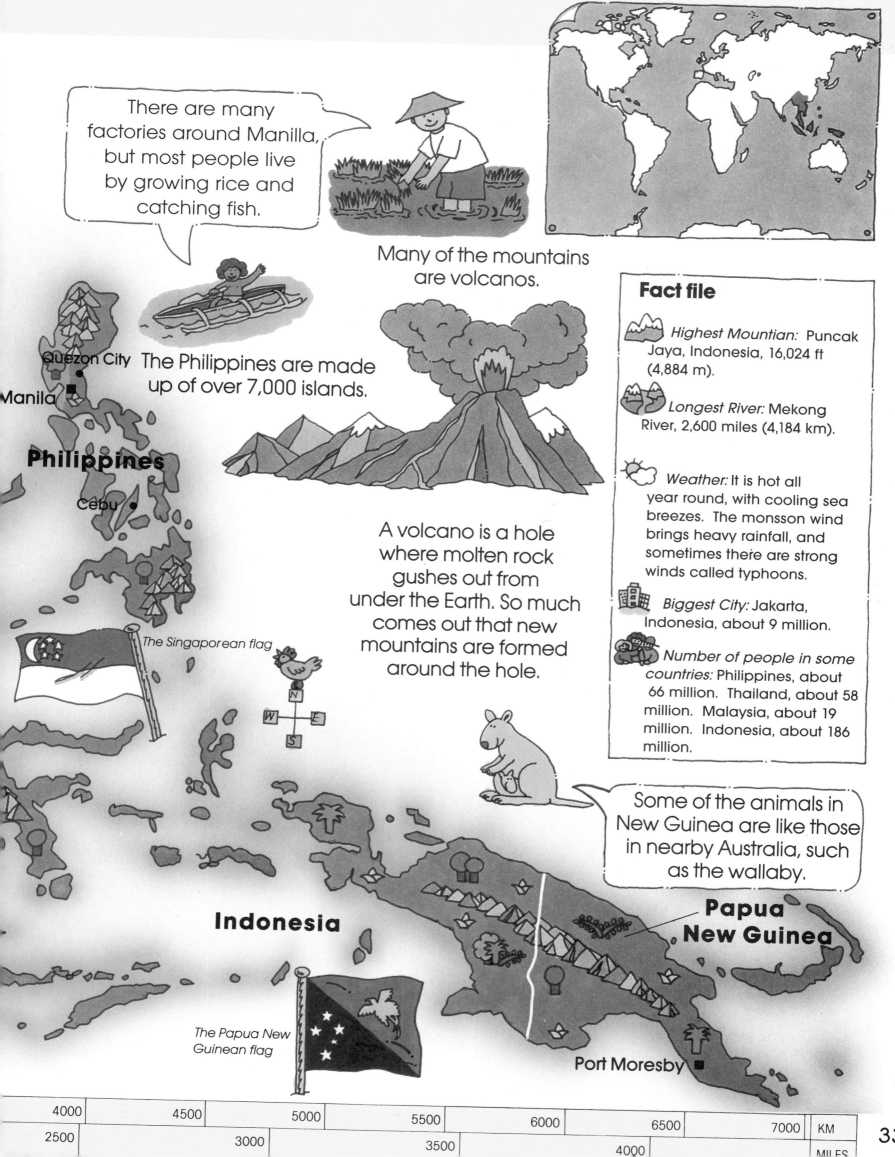

There are many factories around Manilla, but most people live by growing rice and catching fish.

Many of the mountains are volcanos.

The Philippines are made up of over 7,000 islands.

Philippines

Quezon City •

Manila ■

Cebu •

The Singaporean flag

A volcano is a hole where molten rock gushes out from under the Earth. So much comes out that new mountains are formed around the hole.

Fact file

Highest Mountian: Puncak Jaya, Indonesia, 16,024 ft (4,884 m).

Longest River: Mekong River, 2,600 miles (4,184 km).

Weather: It is hot all year round, with cooling sea breezes. The monsson wind brings heavy rainfall, and sometimes there are strong winds called typhoons.

Biggest City: Jakarta, Indonesia, about 9 million.

Number of people in some countries: Philippines, about 66 million. Thailand, about 58 million. Malaysia, about 19 million. Indonesia, about 186 million.

Some of the animals in New Guinea are like those in nearby Australia, such as the wallaby.

Papua New Guinea

Indonesia

The Papua New Guinean flag

Port Moresby ■

| 4000 | 4500 | 5000 | 5500 | 6000 | 6500 | 7000 | KM |
| 2500 | 3000 | 3500 | 4000 | MILES |

East Asia

China is the third largest country in the world. Japan is much smaller, about the same size as Britain, but it is the richest country in Asia.

Chinese temples and pagodas have tiled roofs that curl up at the corners.

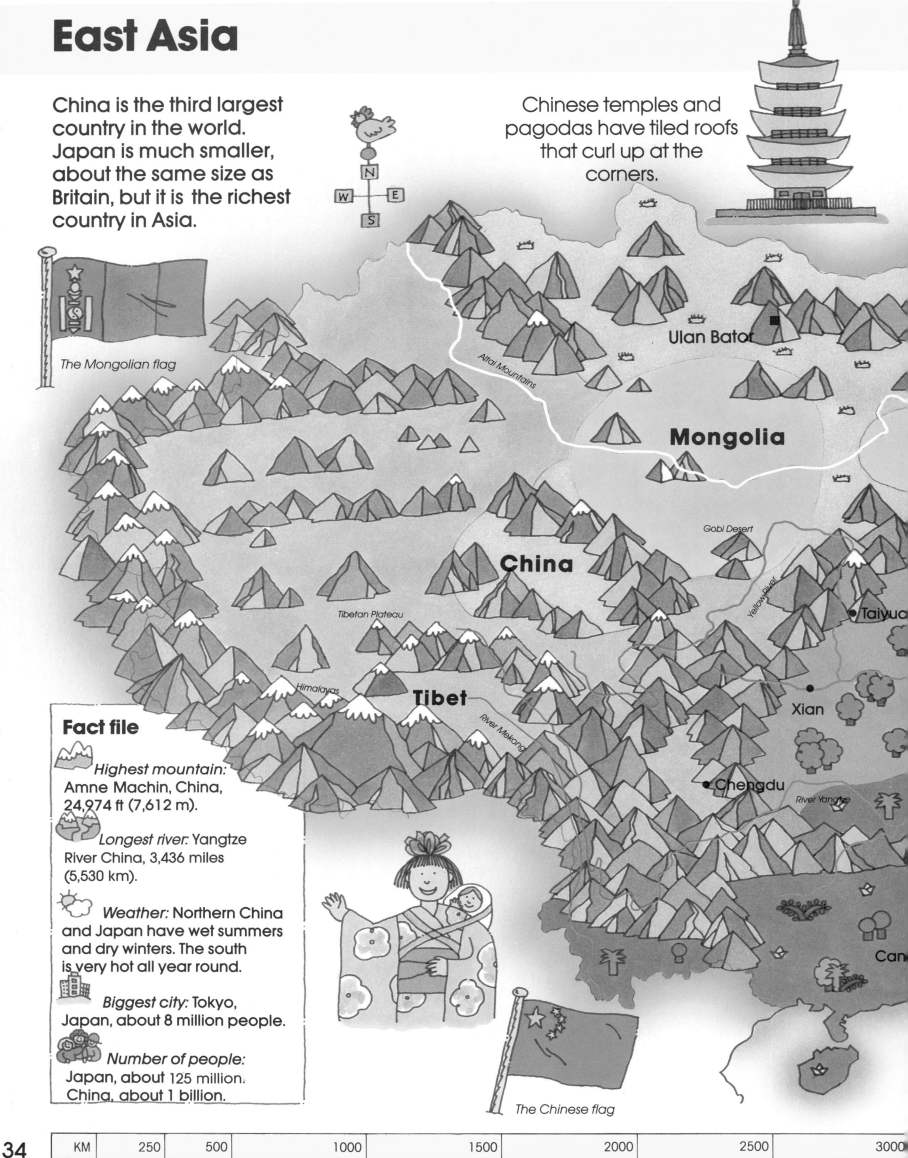

The Mongolian flag

Mongolia

Ulan Bator

Altai Mountains

Gobi Desert

China

Yellow River

Tibetan Plateau

• Taiyua

Himalayas

Tibet

River Mekong

Xian

• Chengdu

River Yangtze

Can

Fact file

Highest mountain: Amne Machin, China, 24,974 ft (7,612 m).

Longest river: Yangtze River China, 3,436 miles (5,530 km).

Weather: Northern China and Japan have wet summers and dry winters. The south is very hot all year round.

Biggest city: Tokyo, Japan, about 8 million people.

Number of people: Japan, about 125 million. China, about 1 billion.

The Chinese flag

KM	250	500	1000	1500	2000	2500	3000
MILES		250	500	1000		1500	

Japan has many factories where people make cars, computers, and televisions.

The Japanese flag

Sea of Japan

Hokkaido

The ancient kingdom of Korea was divided into North and South Korea after the Second World War.

River Amur

• Harbin

• Shen-yang

North Korea

Pyongyang ■

Seoul ■

South Korea

ijing

Hiroshima

Tokyo ■

Kyoto •

Japan

Yellow Sea

Nanjing

Nagasaki

Pacific Ocean

Shanghai •

The Great Wall of China was built over 2,000 years ago to keep out enemies. It winds 1,500 miles (2,414 km) across the hills of northern China.

Rice is grown in paddy fields. These are fields that are flooded by the rains or by rivers.

The South Korean flag

Taipei

Taiwan

Hong Kong

The North Korean flag

A quarter of the world's population lives in China.

Bears and a few giant pandas live in the southwest of China.

Australia and New Zealand

Australia is the smallest continent in the world. It lies in the southern Pacific Ocean, on the opposite side of the world from Europe. New Zealand is 900 miles (1,500km) southeast of Australia. Most of Australia is flat and dry. New Zealand is more hilly and green.

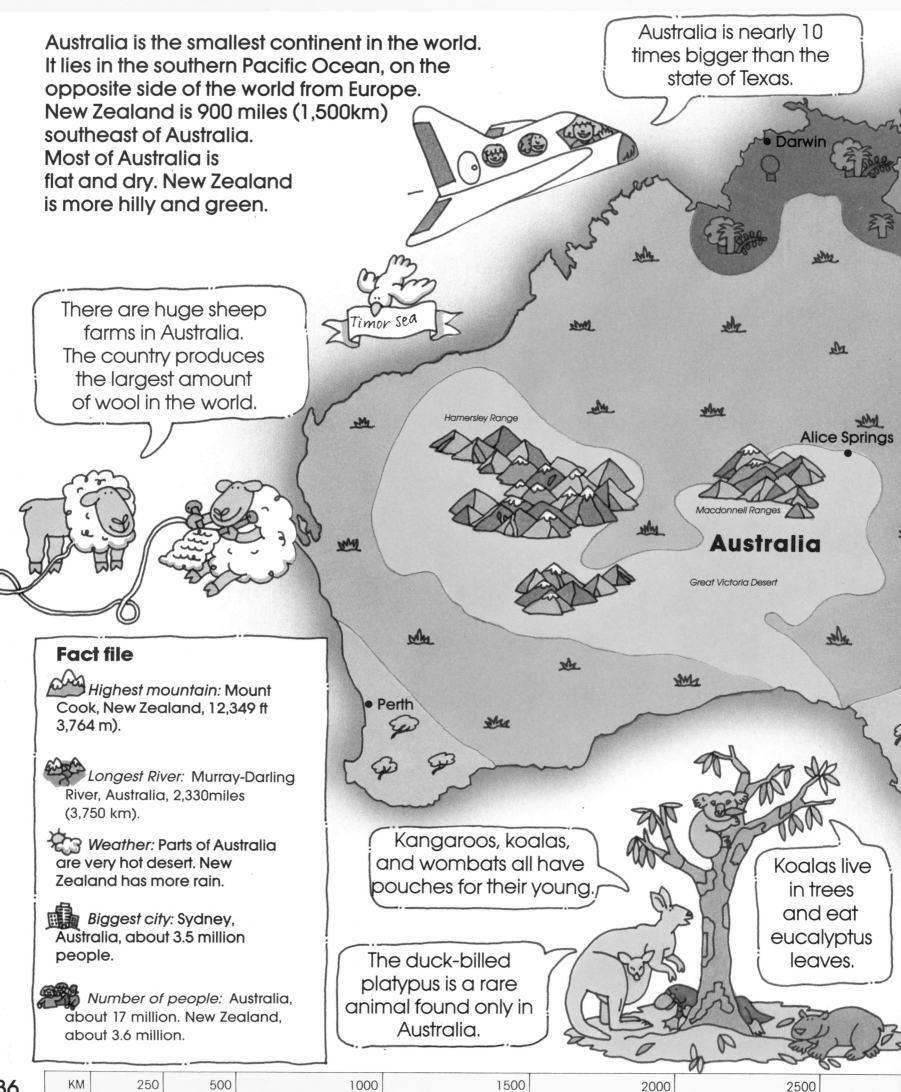

Australia is nearly 10 times bigger than the state of Texas.

There are huge sheep farms in Australia. The country produces the largest amount of wool in the world.

Timor Sea

Hamersley Range

Alice Springs

Macdonnell Ranges

Australia

Great Victoria Desert

Darwin

Perth

Fact file

Highest mountain: Mount Cook, New Zealand, 12,349 ft 3,764 m).

Longest River: Murray-Darling River, Australia, 2,330miles (3,750 km).

Weather: Parts of Australia are very hot desert. New Zealand has more rain.

Biggest city: Sydney, Australia, about 3.5 million people.

Number of people: Australia, about 17 million. New Zealand, about 3.6 million.

Kangaroos, koalas, and wombats all have pouches for their young.

The duck-billed platypus is a rare animal found only in Australia.

Koalas live in trees and eat eucalyptus leaves.

KM	250	500	1000	1500	2000	2500
MILES	250	500	1000	1500		

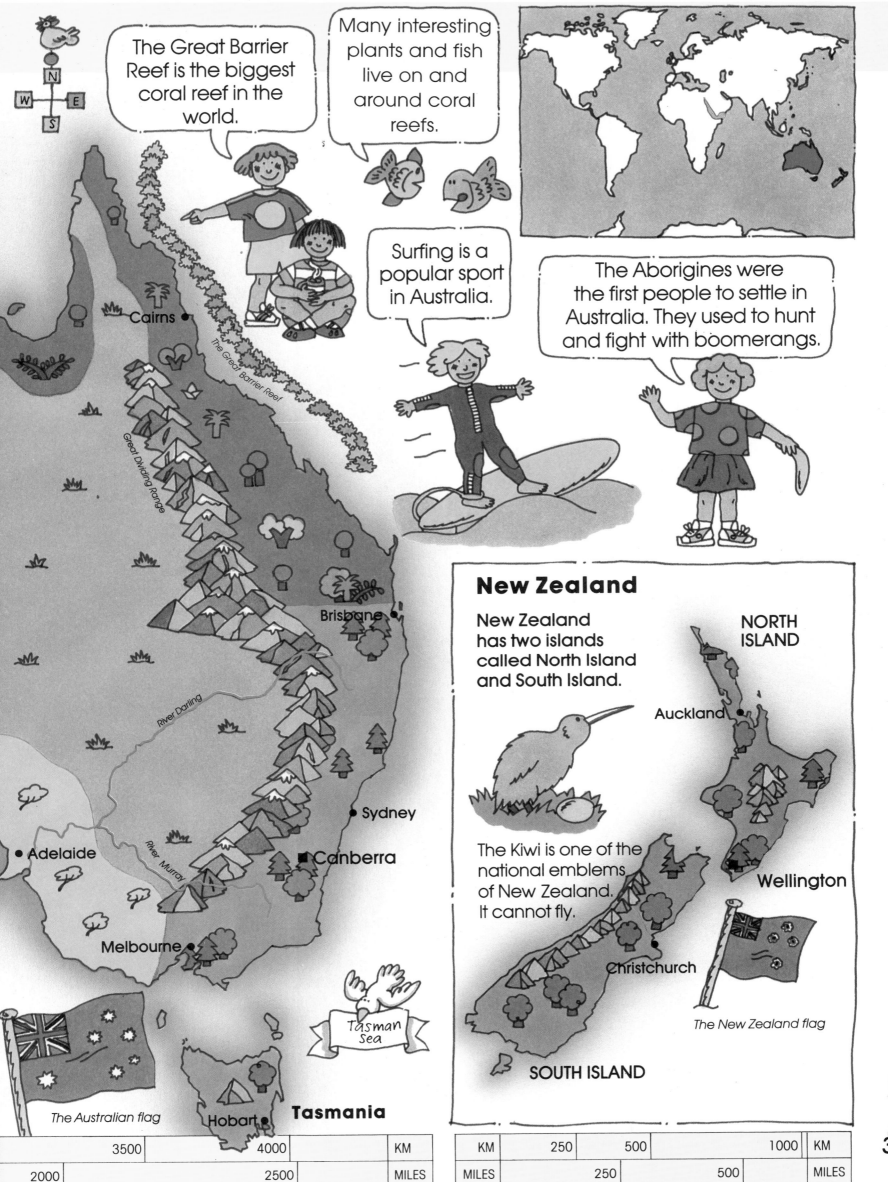

The Great Barrier Reef is the biggest coral reef in the world.

Many interesting plants and fish live on and around coral reefs.

Surfing is a popular sport in Australia.

The Aborigines were the first people to settle in Australia. They used to hunt and fight with boomerangs.

Cairns

The Great Barrier Reef

Great Dividing Range

Brisbane

River Darling

River Murray

Sydney

Adelaide

Canberra

Melbourne

The Australian flag

Tasman Sea

Hobart

Tasmania

New Zealand

New Zealand has two islands called North Island and South Island.

NORTH ISLAND

Auckland

The Kiwi is one of the national emblems of New Zealand. It cannot fly.

Wellington

Christchurch

The New Zealand flag

SOUTH ISLAND

| | 3500 | | 4000 | | KM |
| 2000 | | | 2500 | | MILES |

| KM | 250 | | 500 | | 1000 | KM |
| MILES | | 250 | | | 500 | MILES |

37

The Arctic

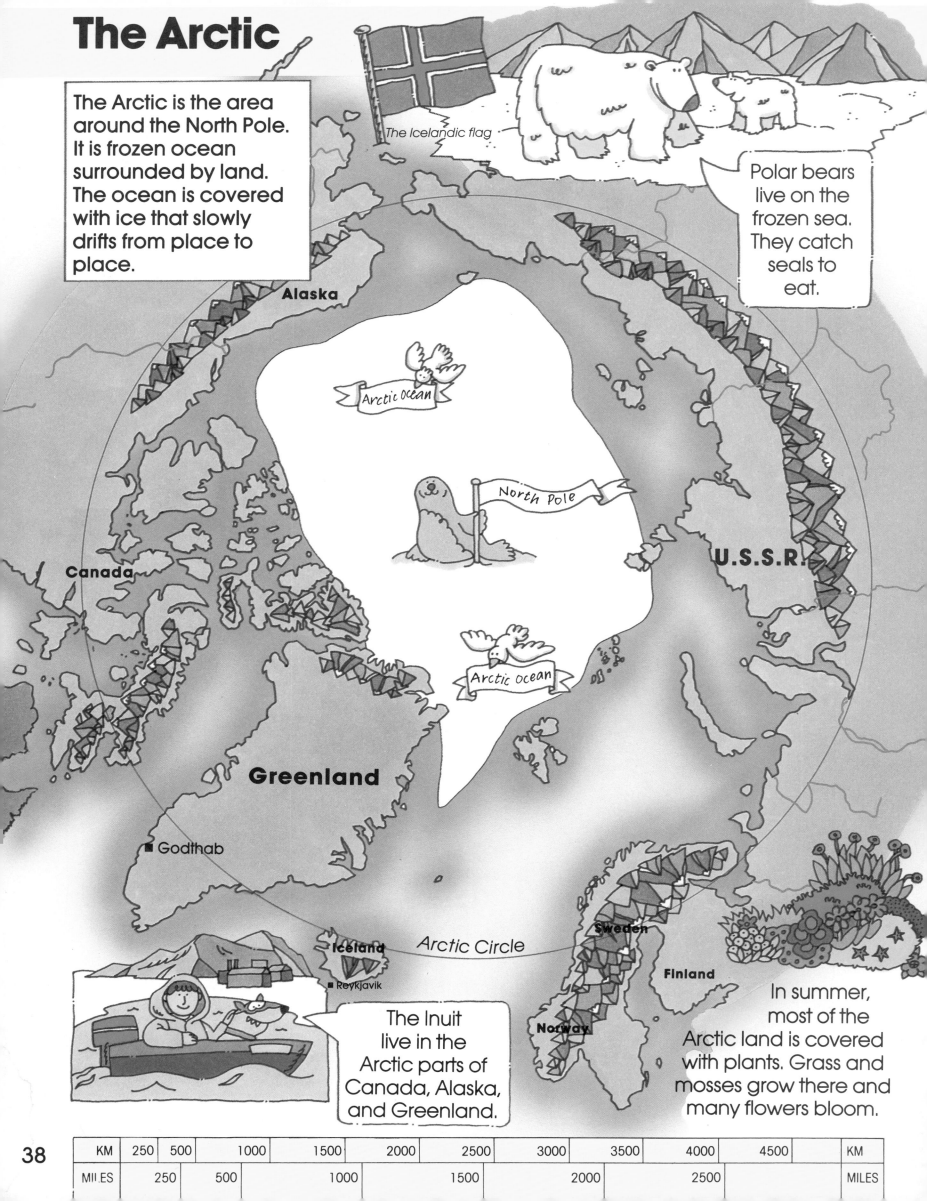

The Arctic is the area around the North Pole. It is frozen ocean surrounded by land. The ocean is covered with ice that slowly drifts from place to place.

The Icelandic flag

Polar bears live on the frozen sea. They catch seals to eat.

Alaska

Arctic Ocean

North Pole

Arctic Ocean

Canada

U.S.S.R.

Greenland

■ Godthab

Sweden

Arctic Circle

Iceland

■ Reykjavik

Finland

Norway

The Inuit live in the Arctic parts of Canada, Alaska, and Greenland.

In summer, most of the Arctic land is covered with plants. Grass and mosses grow there and many flowers bloom.

KM	250	500	1000	1500	2000	2500	3000	3500	4000	4500		KM
MILES		250	500	1000		1500		2000		2500		MILES

The Antarctic

The Antarctic is ice-covered land around the South Pole. The ice is 14,800 feet (4,500 meters) thick in some places. There are many high mountains and some volcanos.

At the North and South Poles, winter and summer last six months each. Winter is dark all day and night. In summer it is light all the time.

The Arctic

The Antarctic

When it is winter at one Pole, it is summer at the other.

Atlantic Ocean

Antarctic Peninsula

South Pole

Amery ice shelf

Antarctic

Transantarctic Mountains

Ross ice shelf

Pacific Ocean

Antarctic Circle

The Antarctic is the coldest place on Earth. The only people living there are scientists.

Whales, fish, birds, and seals live around the coast, but there are no plants or land animals.

Penguins are Antarctic birds. They cannot fly but they swim very well.

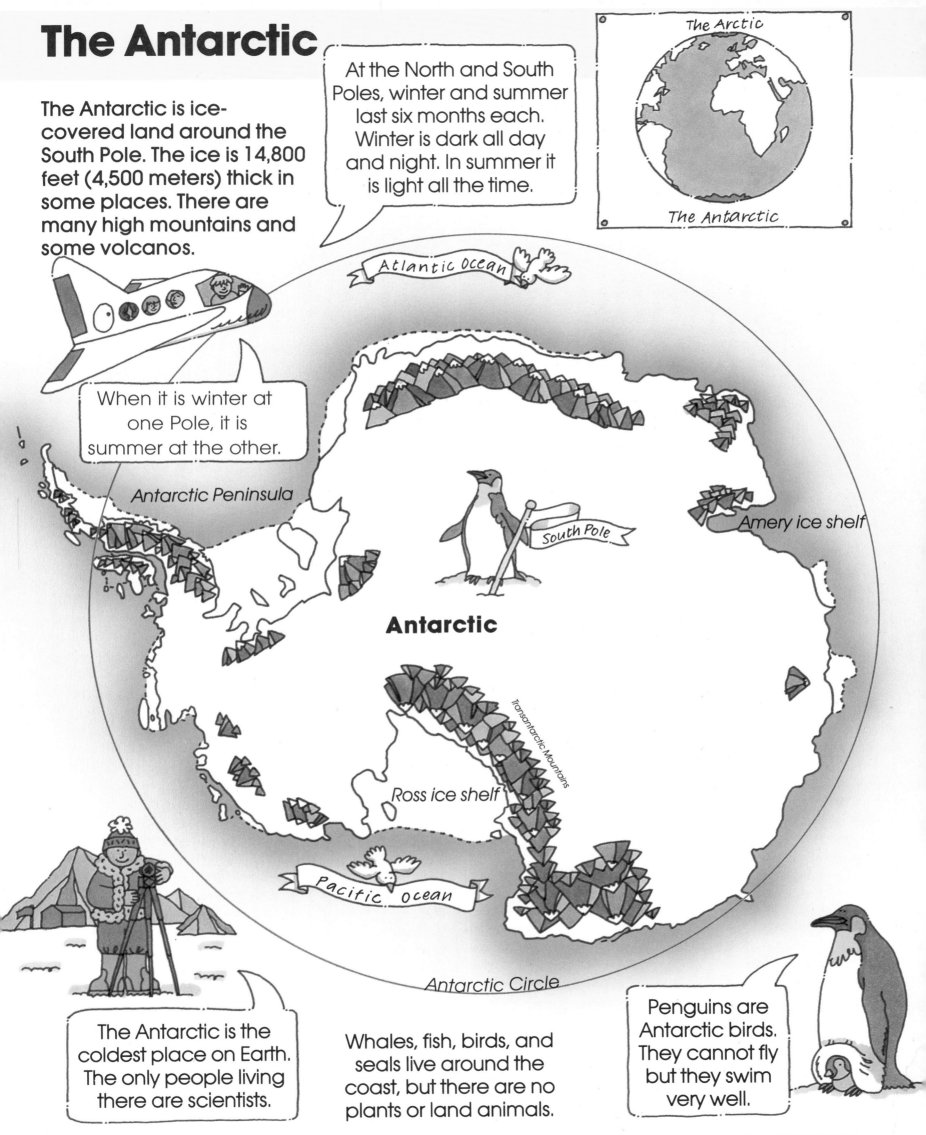

KM	250	500	1000	1500	2000	2500	3000	3500	4000	4500	5000	KM
MILES		250	500	1000		1500		2000		2500		3000	MILES

Index

Afghanistan 29
Alaska 38
Albania 23
Algeria 24
Andorra 22
Angola 24
Antigua & Barbuda 15
Argentina 16
Armenia 26
Australia 28-29
Austria 21
Azerbaijan 26
Bahamas, The 15
Bahrain 29
Bangladesh 31
Barbados 15
Belarus 26
Belgium 20
Belize 15
Benin 24
Bermuda 15
Bhutan 31
Bolivia 16
Bosnia & Herzegovina 23
Botswana 24
Brazil 16
Britain 20
Brunei 32
Bulgaria 21
Burkina Faso 24
Burundi 25
Cambodia 32
Cameroon 24
Canada 14,38
Canary Islands 24
Cape Verde Islands 24
Central African Republic 24
Chad 24
Chile 16
China 34
Colombia 16
Comoro Islands 25
Congo 24
Costa Rica 15
Croatia 23
Cuba 15
Cyprus 28
Czech Republic, The 21
Denmark 18, 20
Djibouti 25
Dominica 15

Dominican Republic 15
Ecuador 16
Egypt 24
El Salvador 15
England 20
Equatorial Guinea 24
Estonia 26
Ethiopia 25
Falkland Islands 16
Finland 19, 38
France 20
French Guiana 16
Gabon 24
Galapagos Islands 16
Gambia, The 24
Georgia 26
Germany 20
Ghana 24
Gibraltar 22
Greece 23
Greenland 38
Grenada 15
Guadeloupe 15
Guatemala 15
Guinea 24
Guinea-Bissau 24
Guyana 16
Haiti 15
Honduras 15
Hong Kong 35
Hungary 21
Iceland 38
India 30
Indonesia 32
Iran 29
Iraq 28
Ireland 20
Israel 28
Italy 23
Ivory Coast 24
Jamaica 15
Japan 35
Jordan 28
Kazakhastan 26
Kenya 25
Kuwait 28
Kyrgyzstan 26
Laos 32
Latvia 26
Lebanon 28
Lesotho 18

Liberia 24
Libya 24
Liechtenstein 20
Lithuania 26
Luxembourg 20
Macedonia 23
Madagascar 25
Madeira Island 24
Malawi 25
Malaysia 32
Mali 24
Malta 23
Martinique 15
Mauritania 24
Mauritius 25
Mexico 14
Moldova 26
Monaco 20
Mongolia 34
Montenegro 23
Morocco 24
Mozambique 25
Myanmar 32
Namibia 24
Nepal 30
Netherlands, The 20
New Zealand 37
Nicaragua 15
Niger 24
Nigeria 24
North Korea 35
Northern Ireland 20
Norway 18, 38
Oman 29
Pakistan 30
Panama 15
Papua New Guinea 33
Paraguay 16
Peru 16
Philippines 33
Poland 21
Portugal 22
Puerto Rico 15
Qatar 29
Romania 21
Russia 26, 38
Rwanda 25
San Marino 23
São Tomé & Príncipe 24
Saudi Arabia 28
Scotland 20

Senegal 24
Serbia 23
Sierra Leone 24
Singapore 32
Slovakia 21
Slovenia 23
Somalia 25
South Africa 24
South Korea 35
Spain 22
Sri Lanka 30
St Kitts-Nevis 15
St Lucia 15
Sudan, The 24
Suriname 16
Swaziland 25
Sweden 18, 38
Switzerland 20
Syria 28
Taiwan 35
Tajikistan 26
Tanzania 25
Thailand 32
Tibet 34
Tobago 15
Togo 24
Trinidad 15
Tunisia 24
Turkey 28
Turkmenistan 26
Uganda 25
Ukraine 26
Uzbekistan 26
United Arab Emirates 29
United States of America
6-13
Uruguay 16
Vatican City 19
Venezuela 16
Vietnam 32
Virgin Islands 15
Wales 20
West Indies 15
Western Sahara 24
Yemen 29
Zaïre 24
Zambia 24
Zimbabwe 25

Copyright © 1991 Quadrillion Publishing Ltd
All rights reserved.

This edition published in 1998 by SMITHMARK Publishers,
a division of U.S. Media Holdings, Inc., 115 West 18th Street,
New York, NY 10011

Produced by ZigZag an imprint of
Quadrillion Publishing Ltd.,
Godalming, Surrey, England,
GU7 1XW

8027
Map consultants: Sussex University Map Library, England
Geography consultants: Diane Snowden, Keith Lye

Color separations by RSC Graphics Ltd., Leeds, England
Printed and bound in Singapore
ISBN 0-7651-9263-2

10 9 8 7 6 5 4 3